Charismatics
Are We
Missing Something?

Charismatics
Are We Missing Something?

by

R. L. Brandt

Distributed by
Logos International
Plainfield, New Jersey

All Scripture quotes are from the King James Version, unless otherwise noted as NEB (The New English Bible).

Lovingly dedicated
to the cherished memory
of my father,
Alfred E. Brandt,
who spent fifty years of his life searching
the Scriptures,
and who
by his sincere love for his Lord
and His Word
was
a source of inspiration to many.

Truth

Great truths are dearly bought, the common truths,
Such as men give and take from day to day,
Come in the common walk of easy life,
Blown by the careless wind across our way.

Great truths are greatly won, not found by chance,
Nor wafted on the breath of summer dream;
But grasped in the great struggle of the soul,
Hard buffeting with adverse wind and stream.

But in the day of conflict, fear and grief,
When the strong hand of God, put forth in might,
Plows up the subsoil of the stagnant heart,
And brings the imprisoned truth seed to the light,

Wrung from the troubled spirit in hard hours,
Of weakness, solitude, perchance of pain,
Truth springs like harvest from the well-plowed field,
And the soul feels it has not wept in vain.

Horatius Bonar

Contents

Preface

From my youth I have been deeply impressed with the idea that truth must be at the top of the list of life's priorities. Anything less than truth is unworthy of man's devotion and energy. Truth must ever be prized as the soul's greatest treasure.

Solomon's weighty words, "Buy the truth, and sell it not," deserve the most careful obedience (Prov. 23:23). While truth may at times bear a high price tag, the dividends will more than compensate for the expenditure.

In my thinking, truth is an absolute without variables. At the precise point that a variable is introduced, truth is diluted. Truth may be conceived of as a perfectly straight line. Man's concept of truth, on the other hand, may well be illustrated by a very uneven line. In certain instances he may possess positive truth. In others he may be a long way off.

There are many obstacles to truth, and none of us escape their influence. To come to the knowledge of the truth is often a painful process. Deep-seated traditions blind our eyes. They must be cut away like cataracts. Longstanding prejudices obstruct the flow of truth and must be purged like malignant tumors. The doctrines of men attach themselves to our minds and hold us in their bondage as though they were the doctrines of God. Such chains are not easily broken.

I think we err and block the entrance of truth when we

fail to recognize the possibility of our own misconceptions. This is the everlasting pitfall of mortal man. Surely the wise man was on key when he wrote, "Every way of a man is right in his own eyes" (Prov. 21:2).

Think for a moment of two New Testament stalwarts, Paul and Peter. Both of these men were hard-nosed dogmatists. And each of them had experiences wherein, in spite of their positive persuasion and dedication, they had to undergo the painful process of being brought into line with truth.

History has seldom, if ever, found a man who was as fully convinced of Christianity's total falsehood as was Saul of Tarsus. His steellike and penetrating mind held no vestige of doubt. He was ready, at any cost, to expend himself for the "truth."

Nevertheless, in the providence of God, a day came wherein Saul discovered, to his own profound embarrass-

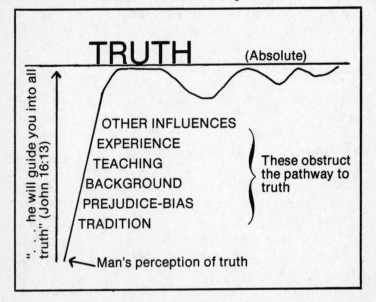

ment and grief, that what he had fully espoused as pure truth was indeed gross error.

Peter was little different. Though he was a devoted disciple, on one occasion he heard the staggering words from his Master, "and when thou art converted, strengthen thy brethren" (Luke 22:32). It is not difficult to guess Peter's thoughts. "Converted? Unthinkable!" Is it possible that one so fully persuaded could possess areas of error? Surely he didn't think so, but his Lord did.

How then shall a man discover and be assured of absolute truth? Must he forever grope in the dark, or is there some way?

I think there are three relatively simple means: (1) an uncompromising willingness to learn, (2) the guidance of the Holy Spirit, and (3) proper attention to the Word of God.

Uncompromising willingness heads the list; for until the will is committed to an acceptance of truth once it is known, it is doubtful it will ever be known. The will of man is perhaps the greatest single deterrent to the truth. It stands at the entrance of the mind, brandishing its flaming sword, and often withstanding the angel of light.

One of the greatest challenges ever placed on mortal man is recorded by John when he quoted the Lord as saying, "If any man will do his will, he shall know of the doctrine, whether it be of God, or whether I speak of myself" (John 7:17). The responsibility for possessing truth, therefore, seems to rest squarely upon the will of man.

Once the will is committed, the second means is quite natural. The Holy Spirit, like a perfect gentleman, will not intrude where He is not welcome. But wherever He is freely received, there He does His work. "Howbeit when he, the Spirit of truth, is come, he will guide you into all truth" (John 16:13).

The third means, though last named, is of prime importance, for by the Word of God, truth is articulated. The Psalmist declared, "Thy word is true" (Ps. 119:160), and Jesus said, "If ye continue in my word, then are ye my disciples indeed; And ye shall know the truth, and the truth shall make you free" (John 8:31-32). In His high priestly prayer, He again stressed this idea when He said, ". . . thy word is truth" (John 17:17).

Truth is as vast as God himself. Therefore no man can ever hope to be the repository of all truth. At best we can only see through a glass darkly.

Nevertheless necessary truth can and must be known.

This book is offered with the prayer of an ancient, "O Lord, save us from the cowardice that shrinks from new truths, from the laziness that is content with half-truths, from the arrogance that thinks it knows all truths."

Charismatics
Are We
Missing Something?

one

On Ignorance and Knowledge

More Pentecostals are alive and in the world today than in all of previous history combined. On the contemporary scene a whole new multitude of charismatics has emerged. Pentecostals and charismatics now saturate every continent on the globe.

Ralph Martin, identified as a Catholic evangelical, is a leader in charismatic renewal. In the March, 1980, issue of *Christianity Today* he stated, "In a recent Gallup survey of American Catholicism, it was reported that 10 percent of American Catholics have had some contact with the charismatic renewal and 8 percent had attended charismatic meetings within the last month. That would mean 5 million American Catholics have had some contact with the charismatic renewal and 4 million actually attended a meeting within the month they were surveyed.

". . . in Colombia there are reported to be more than 10,000 Catholic charismatic prayer groups. In France a few hundred thousand are now involved, and the numbers are growing in many European countries. More than 20 percent of the Irish clergy and nuns have become involved in the charismatic renewal, and the charismatic influence on the Irish celebrations with Pope John Paul II was obvious—in music and in other ways.

"The normal format for charismatic renewal is the small prayer group of 10 to 50 people. There are tens of thousands of these groups all over the world."

This is only a single example of the Pentecostal and charismatic immensity. Somehow the knowledge of the Holy Spirit's availability and readiness to minister to and through ordinary humans has reached these people. In simple faith they have responded, with the result that they have entered an exciting glorious dimension of fresh spiritual experience, having its own contagion.

Yet the vast majority of charismatics and newer Pentecostals will be first to attest their own meager knowledge in relation to the manifestations and gifts of the Holy Spirit. Their zealous pursuit of this knowledge, evidenced by their eager devouring of volumes of books and tapes on the subject, indicates a keen sense of lack and need.

Some observers incline toward doubting the validity of their experience on the grounds that it is more experience oriented than theologically based. J.I. Packer, noted English theologian and professor of systematic and historical theology at Regent College in Vancouver, British Columbia, observed: "Though charismatic Christianity treats experience rather than truth as primary and embraces people with many non-evangelical beliefs, it remains evangelicalism's half-sister; this may explain why evangelical reactions to charismatic renewal seem sometimes to smack of sibling rivalry" (*Christianity Today*, March, 1980).

While it is acknowledged that in the final analysis, experience must bow to sound theology, it must also necessarily be recognized that vital spiritual experience quite commonly predates the individual's broader theological perceptions. This does not mean that his experience is not biblically sound. It simply indicates that his faith, though based upon mere fragments of biblical truth, has launched him into valid and vital spiritual experience.

Obviously, ignorance must be escaped. It is no credit to anyone.

Ever present in charismatic circles, whether in the first-century Church, or now at the end of the age, is the danger that limited knowledge will create serious pitfalls. History flashes its red lights for all to note. There are guidelines to be heeded and taken seriously. Otherwise disappointment and disaster are almost sure to come.

My great concern is with truth—at this point, with what I have chosen to call charismatic truth. That is truth having to do with the Holy Spirit, His manifestations and His gifts. First I covet it for myself. And, second, I covet it in all its fullness for all my fellow charismatics.

It should be noted that Paul's major concern in writing to the early Church charismatics was to impart that knowledge of truth which would eventuate in the most profitable manifestation of spiritual gifts for building up the Church. There is no evidence he ever toyed with the idea of banishing any of these manifestations. Nevertheless, recognizing the inherent danger in the unwise and untaught manifestation of the spiritual gifts, he did set out to lay a solid base of spiritual knowledge whereby faith could be governed and practice could be most meaningful.

The gifts of the Spirit, manifested humbly, are an incomparable force for the good of the Church. But manifested without love they can work more harm than good. "Though I speak with the tongues of men and of angels, and have not charity [love], I am become as sounding brass, or a tinkling symbol" (1 Cor. 13:1).

Error springs from either deception or ignorance. And deception takes advantage of ignorance.

3

I have personally witnessed some of the unhappy fruit of ignorance in the area of utterance gifts. However, unfortunate cases and abuses such as the Corinthian charismatics practiced are not to be construed as proof of unreality of spiritual gifts. They simply underscore the awful importance of our hasting to escape ignorance by diligent and dedicated pursuit of sound knowledge.

Knowledge is the supreme need. Its value is immeasurable. "And by knowledge shall the chambers be filled with all precious and pleasant riches. A wise man is strong; yea, a man of knowledge increaseth strength" (Prov. 24:4-5). "Therefore my people are gone into captivity, because they have no knowledge: and their honourable men are famished, and their multitude dried up with thirst" (Isa. 5:13).

In the vast field of charismatic involvement the number-one need is knowledge. That was the need in Corinth, and that is the need now. "Now concerning spiritual gifts, brethren, I would not have you ignorant" (1 Cor. 12:1). The Corinthians, like modern charismatics, surely had the spiritual gifts. "Ye come behind in no gift" (1 Cor. 1:7). "Ye are zealous of spiritual gifts" (1 Cor. 14:12). But they lacked the know-how for the most meaningful manifestation of those gifts.

Therefore Paul wrote to them as he did in 1 Corinthians 12 through 14. He saw ignorance as an enemy to be reckoned with and eliminated. He perceived it could spell the undoing not only of the gifts, but of the Church itself. He understood the inherent weakness in ignorance, and underscored the importance of escaping it: "When I was a child, I spake as a child, I understood as a child, I thought as a child: but when I became a man, I put away childish things" (1 Cor. 13:11). "Brethren, be not children in understanding" (1 Cor. 14:20).

Paul also understood that knowledge has an important relation to faith, that without it faith is impossible. "How shall they believe in him of whom they have not heard?" he asked the Romans (10:14). Until knowledge comes men cannot believe. "So then faith cometh by hearing" (that is, by the entrance of knowledge—10:17). Ignorance imposes severe limitations. It is a robber and a destroyer. A poster in a classroom for airline pilots read, "What you don't know won't hurt you, it will kill you!" Ignorance is always the enemy of faith.

Knowledge is extremely important. Our faith is wholly dependent on it, just as a skyscraper is dependent on bedrock. This explains Paul's passion that Christians may know. At least five times in his epistles his overwhelming concern that God's people might escape their ignorance surfaces. And each time the cry is almost identical.

"For I would not, brethren, that ye should be ignorant" (Rom. 11:25).

"Moreover, brethren, I would not that ye should be ignorant" (1 Cor. 10:1).

"Now concerning spiritual gifts, brethren, I would not have you ignorant" (1 Cor. 12:1).

"For I would not, brethren, have you ignorant" (2 Cor. 1:8).

"But I would not have you to be ignorant, brethren" (1 Thess. 4:13).

In harmony with his concerns over areas of ignorance, he sought to dispel that ignorance by every possible means. He prayed, he wrote, and he taught. At the heart of every prayer in Ephesians, Philippians and Colossians is an intense plea for knowledge. "That ... God ... may give unto you the spirit of wisdom and revelation in the knowledge of him ... that ye may know" (Eph. 1:17-18).

5

"That he would grant you . . . that ye may be able to comprehend . . . and to know" (Eph. 3:16, 18-19). ". . . that your love may abound yet more and more in knowledge" (Phil. 1:9). ". . . that ye might be filled with the knowledge of his will in all wisdom and spiritual understanding . . . increasing in the knowledge of God" (Col. 1:9-10).

Through the written and Spirit-enlightened Word the believer comes to knowledge, and, once knowledge is at hand, faith can spring up.

Faith, in turn, determines spiritual experience, and experience sets the bounds for ministry. Thus the order is: 1) knowledge, 2) faith, 3) experience, and 4) ministry. And that order is fixed. Knowledge is the starting point in the stairway to effective spiritual ministry. Never faith. Faith presupposes knowledge and precedes spiritual experience. Spiritual experience is the steppingstone to spiritual ministry.

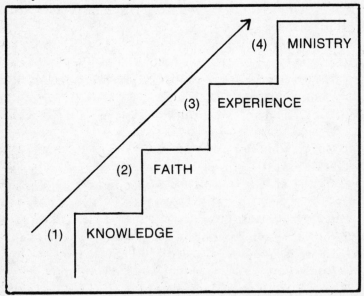

Take Apollos's experience in Acts 18. In the midst of his highly complimentary pedigree is a significant line, "knowing only the baptism of John" (Acts 18:25). Even a casual perusal of the text indicates that his level of knowledge determined the level of his faith, which then governed the level of his experience, which finally circumscribed the bounds of his ministry.

Fortunately Aquila and Priscilla came his way and perceiving his limitations "they took him unto them, and expounded unto him the way of God more perfectly" (Acts 18:26). They imparted knowledge he had not received before. We wonder how his knowledge remained so limited. Over twenty years had passed since the Resurrection, the Ascension, and Pentecost, and yet it appears doubtful whether he had more than a smattering of New Testament understanding. It is quite likely that he understood nothing of the Holy Spirit's present ministry. Some scholars believe the Ephesian believers of Acts 19 were his disciples. If so, they reflected his limited knowledge in their response to Paul, "We have not so much as heard whether there be any Holy Ghost" (Acts 19:2).

We need not be too surprised at this, for now, nearly twenty centuries later, ignorance relating to the Holy Spirit, His manifestation and gifts, remains widespread.

Aquila and Priscilla were effective. Before they finished with Apollos his heart was flooded with new light. His faith rose in beautiful response, leading him into vast new dimensions of spiritual experience, which, in turn resulted in a greatly enhanced ministry. "For he mightily convinced the Jews, and that publickly, shewing by the scriptures that Jesus was Christ" (Acts 18:28).

Added knowledge launched Apollos into a whole new field of spiritual enrichment and more effective ministry. Had it not happened, both he and his world would have been the poorer for it.

We charismatics are in similar shoes. We have some spiritual knowledge. We have vital and to-be-coveted spiritual experience. But unless our base of knowledge is broadened, we will find ourselves in a state of perpetual spiritual infancy. Ignorance imposes its own penalty, but knowledge opens doors to limitless heights.

two

Tongues, the Greatest Gift

Debate over comparative greatness of spiritual gifts is a bit like debate over the issues of Calvinism and Arminianism. It will never be settled to everyone's satisfaction. For a long time we have been told that tongues is the least of the gifts, and we have almost bought that line. Even a charismatic friend had that idea when he said to me, "After all, tongues is the least of the gifts."

While we never cease hearing that tongues speaking is for the carnal and the immature, and is of relatively little importance, it can be shown that in at least several respects it is the greatest of the gifts. Could it be that because of its intended meaningfulness it has suffered such unrelenting debasement?

Arguments for its being least of the gifts are loudly propounded.

The assumption is that since tongues is last named in Paul's listing in 1 Cor. 12:8-10, it must be the least important. "For to one is given by the Spirit the word of wisdom; to another the word of knowledge by the same Spirit; To another faith by the same Spirit; to another the gifts of healing by the same Spirit; To another the working of miracles; to another prophecy; to another discerning of spirits; to another divers kinds of tongues; to another the interpretation of tongues." In 1 Cor. 12:28-30 we see tongues listed last again, "And God hath set some in the church, first apostles, secondarily prophets, thirdly teachers, after that miracles, then gifts of healings, helps, governments, diversities of tongues. Are all apostles? are all prophets? are all teachers? are all workers of miracles? Have all the gifts of healing? do all speak with tongues? do all interpret?"

However, before accepting this view as conclusive some additional evidence should be examined.

From a purely logical point of view the prevailing assumption leaves some problems unresolved.

Applying the same logic to 1 Cor. 13:13, "And now abideth faith, hope, charity, these three," the conclusion is that charity is the least of the virtues. Yet, by no mental maneuver could anyone arrive at such a conclusion, in the face of the text itself, for it concludes with, "but the greatest of these is charity."

What of prophecy? Some insist it is the greatest gift, and not without some reason, for Paul wrote, "Follow after charity and desire spiritual gifts, but rather [most of all] that ye may prophesy . . . for greater is he that prophesieth than he that speaketh with tongues" (1 Cor. 14:1, 5).

Yet, if prophecy is the greatest, why is it not, following the same pattern of logic, named first in 1 Cor. 12:8-10? There it is named sixth.

From the best evidence available, comparing Scripture with Scripture, there is little to indicate that order of listing was meant to establish comparative greatness.

Some teach that greatness as related to spiritual manifestations is a relative thing. That is, that the greatness of one gift above another gift is determined not by the gift itself but by the circumstance to which it is applied. Certainly the idea has merit.

Others hold that tongues speaking is least of the gifts

because it was most prevalant among the barely-escaped-from-heathenism Corinthian church. However, such a view is totally incompatable with Paul's comments: "I would that ye all spake with tongues" (1 Cor. 14:5), and "I thank my God, I speak with tongues more than ye all" (1 Cor. 14:18). In no other instance did Paul project such intense desire that believers might manifest a certain gift. Never did he say, "I would that ye all had the word of wisdom," or the word of knowledge, or another of the gifts. He did generalize by exhorting the Corinthians to "covet earnestly the best gifts" (1 Cor. 12:31), but only regarding his concern that they all would speak with tongues did he particularize. The very least conclusion is that he deemed tongues speaking of vital importance to every believer.

As already indicated, it is doubtful that there will ever be major agreement on which is the greatest gift. The past three-fourths of a century of Pentecostal history demonstrates this, but there is some substantial evidence supporting the idea that, at least in several respects, tongues is the greatest gift.

Before considering this evidence we should evaluate the traditional concept of the various types of tongues speaking. Large segments of the Pentecostal world have long held that there are three particular types of tongues speaking. While it is generally agreed all tongues speaking is the same in essence—that is, that it is supernatural speaking through the influence of the Holy Spirit—it is commonly thought that there is *first* the tongues speaking which is labeled "initial physical evidence." Then, *second*, there is another type of tongues speaking which is for private use. Charismatics call it their prayer language. It should be observed here that neither of the afore-mentioned manifestations of tongues is considered the gift. *Thirdly,* it is held that the gift of tongues is the correct biblical label for tongues speaking which is to be interpreted by manifestation of the gift of interpretation, and which is in the form of a message to the church.

The renowned British charismatic Bible scholar Donald Gee held this view. "It should always be clearly remembered that there is a distinction between Tongues as a 'Sign' and Tongues as a 'Gift.' The former is for 'all' (Acts 2:4); the latter is not for 'all' (1 Cor. 12:30). It is a mistake not to expect all to speak with tongues when receiving a personal Scriptural Pentecostal Experience; it is an equal mistake to unreasonably expect all to speak with Tongues as a matter of exercising a recognized Gift in the Church."[1]

However, this traditional point of view overlooks some evidence for a somewhat different view. At this point it appears to me there is but one gift of tongues which encompasses the whole field of tongues speaking,

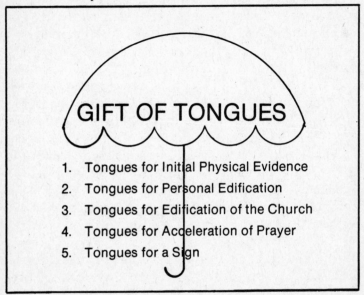

GIFT OF TONGUES

1. Tongues for Initial Physical Evidence
2. Tongues for Personal Edification
3. Tongues for Edification of the Church
4. Tongues for Acceleration of Prayer
5. Tongues for a Sign

which includes as many as five different facets: 1) tongues which occur at the time of baptism with the Holy Spirit, 2) tongues for personal edification, 3) tongues for edification of the body, 4) tongues for praying (which may be included under personal edification but which performs a function beyond personal edification), and 5) tongues for a sign.

I note that Harold Horton, another British charismatic scholar, seems to concur with this view, for he writes of tongues, "It is the *Gift* that is manifested in each case when believers receive their Baptism in the Holy Spirit, though other gifts may be manifested as well: it is therefore often in evidence."[2]

There are some definite reasons for this view.

It has been quite commonly thought and taught that in Paul's statement, "For he that speaketh in an unknown tongue speaketh not unto men, but unto God" (1 Cor. 14:2), he was not thinking of the gift of tongues, but that he was mindful rather, at this instant, of tongues for personal edification, which is not considered the gift of tongues.

Now this view is quite necessary if the traditional "message in tongues" concept is held. The "message in tongues" concept holds that through the gift of tongues God speaks to the Church. Therefore, in this line of reason, Paul here cannot be writing of the "gift," but rather of something other than the "gift."

The same rationale is applied to other Pauline statements in 1 Corinthians 14: "For if I pray in an unknown tongue, my spirit prayeth, but my understanding is unfruitful. What is it then? I will pray with the spirit, and I will pray with the understanding also: I will sing with the spirit, and I will sing with the understanding also" (vv. 14 and 15).

13

This traditional view, however, poses some hermeneutical problems. It has always interested me to note how much of biblical interpretation is governed by certain requirements which experience or tradition dictate. A certain interpretation does not fit some solidly entrenched idea, with the result that the only acceptable interpretation is that which supports the fixed idea. But truth can hardly bow at such an altar.

One of the most elementary laws of hermeneutics is that a text must always be interpreted in the light of its context. Applying this to Paul's discussion of tongues in 1 Corinthians 14, it is both sound and safe to hold that Paul, though he says that "he that speaketh in an unknown tongue, speaketh not unto men but unto God," and though he states, "I will pray with the spirit . . . and I will sing with the spirit," is most certainly speaking about the gift of tongues. In his introduction of the subject under consideration in 1 Corinthians 12 through 14, he makes it unmistakably clear that his subject is specifically the spiritual gifts: "Now concerning spiritual gifts . . . I would not have you ignorant" (1 Cor. 12:1).

Admittedly "gifts" is added by the translators. A more accurate translation would be "Now concerning spirituals." "Spirituals" is obviously a reference to manifestations of the Spirit. Therefore, "manifestations" might be a more suitable word than "gifts." However, the word "gift" does no violence to the idea being conveyed, for later in the passage Paul says, "For to one is given." That which is given can rightly be labeled a "gift." And it should be noted that in the list of spirituals, including all the other recognized gifts or manifestations, tongues is also included, followed by interpretation. Thus, when reference is made to tongues in what follows (chapters 12-14), it is necessary to recognize that it falls under the categorization of the gift of tongues.

14

Consequently, to insist that he is not speaking of the "gift of tongues" merely because some of his statements do not coincide with the traditional concept of that gift is to set our sails in a direction fraught with dangers.

There is another consideration. When Paul ministered to the dozen or some new disciples at Ephesus, as recorded in Acts 19, "the Holy Ghost came on them; and they spake with tongues, and prophesied" (v. 6). What was this prophesying which they did? It would be difficult to argue that this was not a manifestation of the supernatural gift of prophecy. Yet, when one concedes this was the gift of prophecy, he is almost compelled to accept the idea that the tongues speaking on that occasion was a manifestation of the gift of tongues. It would be quite inconsistent to hold that the prophesying was the gift of prophecy and that the tongues speaking was not the gift of tongues.

Finally, Paul's admonition in 1 Cor. 14:28 to the speaker in tongues deserves careful note: "If there be no interpreter, let him keep silence in the church; let him speak to himself, and to God." The instruction is clear. If there is no interpreter present, the tongues speaker is to speak under his breath so as not to be heard publicly, and so only God can hear him. But if, as is commonly believed, the tongues speaking which is meant to be interpreted is a message from God to the people, what is the sense of speaking it to God? That would be tantamount to God speaking to himself. More attention will be given to this in a later chapter.

The concept that the gift of tongues is, at least in several respects, the greatest of the gifts is quite well-founded.

First, it is the single gift intended for universal manifestation. While it is true that the Spirit divides to *"every man*

15

severally as he will" (1 Cor. 12:11), it is also true that Paul said, "I would that ye all spake with tongues" (1 Cor. 14:5).

Here the importance of the gift is indicated more by its broadness of availability than by its particular function, the point being that no Christian needs feel the gift is not for him. The fact is that the gift is so vital and meaningful that all believers can benefit greatly from it.

Further, it is the one gift which can be manifested almost anytime, anywhere, and in any circumstance. It can be manifested in absolute privacy or in the midst of a multitude. It can be employed in life's most desperate circumstances, and also in highest praise to the Creator.

The gift of tongues is the one gift, of the nine mentioned in 1 Corinthians 12, which is intended for personal edification. Surely this makes it greater than all the other gifts as related to the individual.

Then, too, it is in a special sense the kindergarten of the supernatural. The Spirit-controlled life is a life in the supernatural. The gift of tongues is the launching pad for this life. How difficult it is for all of us to move out of the natural into the supernatural. Tongues is a God-appointed means for this.

In the same vein of thought, tongues is the starter-gift. Those who have visited Israel have no doubt observed the everywhere-present souvenir candlesticks. The candlestick to Israel is a most significant symbol. The curious thing is that there are two different kinds of candlesticks—a candlestick with seven candles and a candlestick with nine candles. Each has its own significance to the Jewish community.

But there is a noteworthy difference. While the seven candles of the first kind of candlestick are solidly fixed in position, the nine candles of the other candlestick have

16

one candle which is not solidly fixed. It is very much a part of the whole, but it is removable. The reason is that the free candle is first lighted, and with it, the other eight are lighted subsequently.

The gift of tongues is to the eight other gifts what the free candle is to the other eight. It is most assuredly a part of the whole, but it has its own special function, for by it all of the others are launched into their particular functions.

A glance at the evident chronology of the gifts of the Spirit as portrayed in the Acts lends credence to the view stated above. On the day of Pentecost men, for the first time in the Church age, were baptized in the Holy Spirit. They were then and there introduced to a whole new level of spiritual experience, and as they entered into it they found themselves, first of all, speaking in other tongues. The "starter candle," tongues speaking, was lighted. Then came the other gifts: prophecy (evident in Peter's sermon in Acts 2:14-36), the gifts of healing (Acts 3:1-8), the word of knowledge, possibly the word of wisdom, the gift of miracles, and the gift of faith, all discernible in the account of Ananias and Sapphira (Acts 5:1-11).

At the house of Cornelius, again the first of the gifts to be manifested was the gift of tongues, and also at Ephesus, where the further gift of prophecy was present. The chronology is the same—first tongues, then prophecy.

Again, *tongues speaking is the language of the spirit.* Paul said, "I will pray with the spirit . . . I will sing with the spirit" (1 Cor. 14:15). The highest communication is in the spirit. How beautiful is that communication of the sanctified human spirit, played upon by the Holy Spirit, enabling it to communicate freely with the Father of spirits. "Montanus truly said that each human spirit is like a harp, which the Holy Spirit strikes as with a

17

plectrum, and which yields itself to the mighty hand by which the chords are swept" *(The Pulpit Commentary).* [3]

Blessed escape from spiritual muteness!

Tongues speaking is a mighty weapon for our warfare. "For though we walk in the flesh, we do not war after the flesh; (For the weapons of our warfare are not carnal, but mighty through God to the pulling down of strong holds;) Casting down imaginations, and every high thing that exalteth itself against the knowledge of God, and bringing into captivity every thought to the obedience of Christ" (2 Cor. 10:3-5).

We have yet to discover to the fullest extent what an effective weapon the gift of tongues is in our spiritual warfare. The amassed armies of the enemies are put to flight by this means.

Somehow we have not fully perceived how vital prayer in the spirit is to our successful warfare. But Paul perceived it. In concluding his discussion with the Ephesians relative to the believer's warfare and weaponry, he places the capstone by instructing: "Praying always with all prayer and supplication in the Spirit" (Eph. 6:18). This praying is not separate from the believer's weaponry. Rather, it is the most vital part of all. As the end of the age approaches, we need to understand this.

A final reason for the greatness of the gift of tongues is the fact that *it is the worship gift.* There is no higher spiritual exercise than worship, and there is no higher means of worship than worship in the spirit through tongues speaking.

Surely the enemy of the Church has gained a great victory by relegating tongues to the position of the least of the gifts. The psychological impact of such a view leaves a sense of the gift's utter unimportance. And because men consider it unimportant they are prone not to concern themselves with it. How unfortunate!

We can learn a great lesson from Jewish legend relating to the building of the Temple in Jerusalem.

When the Temple was under construction no sound of a hammer was heard at the building site, the reason being that the stones were quarried elsewhere and brought to the site when they were perfectly shaped and ready for laying.

The legend has it that at one point in the project a stone arrived on the building site which did not seem to fit anywhere. "Since being in the way, it was laboriously moved over to the eastern edge of the temple area, and tumbled down into the Kidron Valley."[4]

Years later the need arose for a most important stone, but it was not to be found. Inquiry was made to the quarrymen, and the answer came back, "That stone was sent up long ago."

Then some of the older workmen remembered. A stone had indeed arrived on the site, but since there seemed to be no place for it, it was relegated to the garbage dump. Thereupon a search was made, and sure enough, there it was, grown over with vines on the slopes of Kidron.

Once again it was moved to the building site, where it fit the need perfectly. And then "The stone which the builders rejected, the same is become the head of the corner" (Matt. 21:42).

The gift of tongues has been treated much like the rejected stone. The Great Quarryman sent it to the "building site" where another Temple is under construction. But it didn't seem to fit. The "builders" decided it was unimportant and that it was for another day. So they relegated it to "Kidron Valley," the place of debris, where it has been all but forgotten.

Men have thought it was of little consequence. "But

19

God hath chosen the foolish things of the world to confound the wise; and God hath chosen the weak things of the world to confound the things which are mighty; and base things of the world, and things which are despised, hath God chosen, yea, and things which are not, to bring to naught things that are: that no flesh should glory in his presence" (1 Cor. 1:27-29).

Hence that which has been deemed unimportant and of little consequence in the eyes of men may be among the most meaningful of the gifts.

Most certainly, the chief of the apostles should be an authority on its greatness and importance. I remind you, he said, "I speak with tongues more than ye all" (1 Cor. 14:18). And he prefaced that remark with "I thank my God."

three

With or Without

Regarding tongues as the initial physical evidence of the Holy Spirit baptism, there are three principle views.

One school of thought holds that the baptism in the Holy Spirit is strictly by faith without any accompanying initial physical evidence such as speaking with tongues.

Another group teaches that when a person is baptized in the Holy Spirit he may or may not speak with tongues.

A third group insists that all who are truly baptized in the Spirit speak with tongues as the initial physical evidence and that there is no exception to this rule.

We shall attempt to examine each of these views with the utmost objectivity and to arrive at a scripturally sound conclusion.

The first of these views is quite broadly subscribed to, particularly by that segment of Christianity which is essentially Calvinistic in theology. The reasons for this might well be pursued by some able scholar. But there are others of vastly different theological persuasion who hold the same view.

As a general rule, those of this persuasion hold that the baptism in the Holy Spirit is received at the precise time when an individual is converted to Christ, or at the time when hands of certain properly designated clergy are laid upon the individual for the express purpose of imparting the Holy Spirit to him.

On the surface there does appear to be some validity

to this view. When Peter had ended his sermon on the day of Pentecost and the men of Israel had responded with their searching inquiry, "Men and brethren, what shall we do?" Peter replied, "Repent and be baptized every one of you in the name of Jesus Christ for the remission of sins, and ye shall receive the gift of the Holy Ghost" (Acts 2:37-38).

Proponents of this first view argue that this passage of Scripture guarantees that all who do repent and are baptized automatically receive the gift of the Holy Ghost.

Commenting on this passage in his book *What About Tongues Speaking?* Anthony Hoekema writes, "At this time Peter said to the multitude, 'Repent, and be baptized every one of you in the name of Jesus Christ for the remission of sins, and ye shall receive the gift of the Holy Ghost' (Acts 2:38). Pentecostals claim that 'the gift of the Holy Spirit,' as here described, means Spirit baptism accompanied by tongues. This is of course a possible interpretation.

"It does not seem likely, however, for two reasons: 1) though we do read that many wonders and signs were done through the apostles (v. 43) we do not read that the three thousand who were converted on the day of Pentecost spoke with tongues; and 2) when thus interpreted, the passage proves too much even for the Pentecostals, since Peter would be implying that the repentance which brings one into possession of the remission of sins is sufficient for the reception of Spirit-baptism—in other words, that all believers automatically receive Spirit-baptism followed by tongues. I prefer to believe with Calvin, Lenski, and Bruce, that 'the gift of the Holy Spirit' here means the Holy Spirit himself as He imparts the blessings of salvation, with no specific reference to charismatic gifts such as glossalalia. When thus understood,

Acts 2 does not prove that every believer must receive a Spirit-baptism some time after he has come to faith. Peter's injunction to the multitude, in fact, rather implies that this is when one repents and believes that he receives the Holy Spirit, not at some later time.' "[5]

It would be folly to argue that this was not God's intent. However, that this is the case in actual practice is demonstrably not necessarily true at all. This is not to accuse God of unfaithfulness in any sense of the word. Rather, it is to admit to man's failure in appropriating God's provision, for one reason or another.

Israel is a valid illustration. Through Moses God made promise to Egypt-enslaved Israel that He would deliver them out of the land of their oppression and bring them into a land flowing with milk and honey. Here is the exact record: "Wherefore say unto the children of Israel, I am the Lord, and I will bring you out from under the burdens of the Egyptians, and I will rid you out of their bondage, and I will redeem you with a stretched out arm, and with great judgments: And I will take you to me for a people, and I will be to you a God: and ye shall know that I am the Lord your God, which bringeth you out from under the burdens of the Egyptians. And I will bring you in unto the land, concerning the which I did swear to give it to Abraham, to Isaac, and to Jacob; and I will give it to you for an heritage: I am the Lord" (Exod. 6:6-8).

Yet, despite this clear declaration of intent and in the face of this unmistakable promise, the Bible records that of the vast Hebrew army to whom God made promise, only two of those who were adults at the time of the escape from Egypt—Caleb and Joshua—ever possessed the Promised Land.

Would anyone dare charge God with infidelity to His promise? "Let God be true, but every man a liar"

(Rom. 3:4). Did not Israel obediently take the first necessary steps of escape via the blood of the sacrificial lamb
and the route through the Red Sea? Why then did not
Israel, which began so well, see complete fulfillment
to God's promise? The answer is recorded in Heb. 4:6,
"They to whom it was first preached entered not in because of unbelief."

Unbelief is the product of the purely human viewpoint.
Israel fell victim to the rationalizing of a few spies, and
wandered in the wilderness for forty years, only to die
short of the divine intention for them.

Even so, there is danger that many of God's children
in modern times suffer even greater loss, not because
God's promises are invalid, but because men have hin-
dered their faith through humanistic rationalizing.

They have begun well. They have indeed repented and
have gone on to water baptism. But then they have confronted certain teachings and dogmas which have set
them going in circles of spiritual nonfulfillment. Their
journey into the Promised Land of the Spirit's fullness is
interrupted and quite possibly ended, and they come far
short of God's gracious intention for them.

To summarize then, the vast majority of Israelites
who followed Moses out of Egypt never did enjoy the
milk and honey and fullness of Canaan, simply because
their faith never carried them into the land. They never
got into the land; therefore they never experienced the
evidences of the land's fullness.

In the same sense spiritually, hosts of God's children
today have received no sign of the fullness of the Spirit,
for the simple reason that their faith has never been able
to surmount the barriers of human rationalization and
carry them into the fullness of the Spirit.

That an individual can repent and be baptized in the

Church age, and yet not be baptized with the Spirit, is quite evident from the account of the Samaritan revival.

Philip had a remarkable ministry of preaching and healing in the city of Samaria. The result was that many believed and were baptized. "But when they believed Philip preaching the things concerning the kingdom of God, and the name of Jesus Christ, they were baptized, both men and women" (Acts 8:12).

Now, it appears that the conditions laid down by Peter for receiving the gift of the Holy Ghost had been fully met. "Repent and be baptized every one of you in the name of Jesus Christ for the remission of sins, and ye shall receive the gift of the Holy Ghost" (Acts 2:38).

Nevertheless, it is apparent they had not received the fullness of the Spirit, "For as yet he was fallen upon none of them: only they were baptized in the name of the Lord Jesus" (Acts 8:10).

Additional help through prayer and ministry was necessary to carry the Samaritans into the fullness of the Spirit. "Now when the apostles which were at Jerusalem heard that Samaria had received the word of God, they sent unto them Peter and John: Who when they were come down, prayed for them, that they might receive the Holy Ghost. . . . Then laid they their hands on them, and they received the Holy Ghost" (Acts 8:14-15, 17).

Thus the point of view that insists all who repent and are baptized in water are baptized in the Holy Ghost does not seem compatible with either the biblical experience nor historical evidence.

A second school of thought holds that the Holy Spirit may be received in His fullness *with or without* the accompanying evidence of tongues speaking.

This position is supported most often with experiential evidence rather than with biblical teaching or example.

It appears to be an accommodation concept which has been developed to comfort and assure those who have not spoken with tongues. To support it by way of sound biblical exegesis is impossible, and to rely upon experience in supporting a doctrinal position of any kind is to open the door to a thousand errors.

Those who espouse the "with or without" view may resort to the five recorded cases in the Acts wherein individuals or groups initially received the Holy Spirit, pointing out that in only three of the five cases did they speak with tongues. The logical conclusion, in this light, would be that the recipient may or may not speak with tongues at the time of receiving.

However, a closer scrutiny of the cases whereof it is not stated that they spoke with tongues, rather than lending support to the "with or without" position, does quite the opposite.

The three recorded cases of tongues speaking in connection with the initial experience of Holy Spirit baptism are Acts 2:4 at Pentecost, "And they were all filled with the Holy Ghost, and began to speak with other tongues, as the Spirit gave them utterance"; Acts 10:44-46 at Cornelius' house, "While Peter yet spake these words, the Holy Ghost fell on all them which heard the word. And they of the circumcision which believed were astonished, as many as came with Peter, because that on the Gentiles also was poured out the gift of the Holy Ghost. For they heard them speak with tongues, and magnify God"; and Acts 19:6 at Ephesus, "And when Paul had laid his hands upon them, the Holy Ghost came on them; and they spake with tongues and prophesied."

The two cases wherein tongues speaking is not recorded are Acts 8:17 at Samaria, "Then laid they their hands on them and they received the Holy Ghost," and

Acts 9:17, when Paul was filled with the Holy Ghost, "And Ananias went his way, and entered into the house; and putting his hands on him said, Brother Saul, the Lord, even Jesus, that appeared unto thee in the way as thou camest, hath sent me, that thou mightest receive thy sight, and be filled with the Holy Ghost." We shall examine these more closely.

At the outset it should be noted that in neither of these cases is there any statement to hint they did not speak with tongues. The "with or without" proponent may assume this, but at the same moment he is compelled to concede the argument proves or disproves nothing, for the proponents of tongues speaking, using the same evidence, can as well assume that the recipients did speak with tongues.

Notwithstanding, other evidence should be examined.

Close scrutiny of Simon the sorcerer will help the earnest inquirer. Simon, by his magical arts, had deluded the Samaritans into thinking he possessed great powers. "But there was a certain man, called Simon, which beforetime in the same city used sorcery, and bewitched the people of Samaria, giving out that himself was some great one: to whom they all gave heed, from the least to the greatest, saying, This man is the great power of God. And to him they had regard, because that of a long time he had bewitched them with sorceries" (Acts 8:9-11).

For Simon, sorcery was no doubt a lucrative business. But when Philip performed genuine miracles and preached Jesus in his city, "Simon himself believed also: and when he was baptized, he continued with Philip, and wondered, beholding the miracles and signs which were done" (Acts 8:13).

Then came Peter and John. As they laid hands on Philip's converts, "They received the Holy Ghost" (Acts 8:17).

Seeing what was happening, Simon was impressed. In fact, so great was his intrigue, he was immediately willing to pay money that he might have the same power as Peter and John had for imparting the Holy Ghost. "And when Simon saw that through laying on of the apostles' hands the Holy Ghost was given, he offered them money, Saying, Give me also this power, that on whomsoever I lay hands, he may receive the Holy Ghost" (Acts 8:18-19).

What did Simon see? That he saw something of unusual proportion is evident.

It should be noted here that there is substantial biblical evidence showing that whenever men are baptized in the Holy Spirit, there will be manifestations that are discernible to the senses.

In speaking of the manifestations on the day of Pentecost, Peter said, "He hath shed forth this which ye now see and hear" (Acts 2:33). In the instance before us Luke records, "And when Simon saw that through the laying on of the apostles hands the Holy Ghost was given . . ." (Acts 8:18). Again at the house of Cornelius there was a visible and audible manifestation, which provoked astonishment on the part of the Jewish witnesses, "For they heard them speak with tongues" (Acts 10:46).

The key to understanding what Simon saw is in Peter's rebuke, "Thy money perish with thee . . . thou hast neither part nor lot in this matter" (Acts 8:20-21).

The word translated "matter" here is, in the Greek, *logos.* It has been translated "teaching," "ministry," or "word" in various Bible versions. The essential meaning is "expression" or "utterance." The particular meaning is determined by the circumstances of its usage. Thus the supportive evidence in this instance points to a clear inference of "supernatural utterance," which would be tongues speaking.

Relating this to Peter's response, it would do no violence to paraphrase, "thou hast neither part nor lot in this supernatural utterance."

The reasonable conclusion then is that when the Samaritans received the Holy Spirit they too spoke with tongues.

Paul's experience recorded in Acts 9 should also be considered.

Following his Damascus road confrontation with Jesus, he was led into the city where he spent three days fasting and praying. During this time a little-known disciple named Ananias was instructed by the Lord to go to the praying Saul of Tarsus "that he might receive his sight and be filled with the Holy Ghost" (Acts 9:17).

The inference is clear that here Paul received his baptism in the Holy Spirit. Yet there is no statement as to whether he spoke with tongues. To argue that he did not would be of no more validity than a similar argument for the Samaritan experience.

However, at a later date Paul himself wrote, "I speak with tongues more than ye all" (1 Cor. 14:18). In the Greek text the idea conveyed is that Paul testified to speaking with tongues more than all the Corinthians put together. When then did he begin? No doubt, when he was baptized in the Spirit.

Thus it is clear that in three of the five recorded instances of baptism in the Spirit they spoke with tongues at the time of receiving. In the other two, while it is not stated in the account, there is substantial evidence that the recipients also spoke with tongues upon receiving.

The three reported biblical cases wherein a statement is given on what actually happened when men received should be sufficient evidence to show the "with or without" position unsupportable by the majority of evidence.

Add to this the evidence for speaking in tongues in the other two instances and you have a solid case averse to the "with or without" position.

Even so, there is yet another Scripture used to support the "with or without" view. It is Paul's question in 1 Cor. 12:30, "do all speak with tongues?" The form of the question calls for an obvious "no" answer. However, the picture clears when it is noted that Paul, in this instance, is not dealing with the initial reception of the Holy Spirit. This experience had already come to the Corinthians, and consequently his concern here is with what follows the initial experience.

In discussing the general function of the various gifts, particularly in the public service, he indicates that not all of the Corinthians were used by God to speak with tongues and interpret.

Thus it is seen that the passage under consideration really does not bear upon the "with or without" question.

Lastly, let us examine the view of those who hold that all who are genuinely filled with the Holy Spirit do speak with tongues at the time of their initial experience. Is this a valid view, and can it stand the test of careful Bible-oriented scrutiny?

There are at least three incontrovertible defenses for this position.

First is the reason of precedent. Webster defines precedent as something previously said or done, serving as an example to be followed.

No more meaningful and pure precedent for initial physical evidence exists than the very first reception of the Holy Spirit on the day of Pentecost. There men were not influenced by preconceived ideas, nor inhibited by human rationalizations. They had no previous experience to hint at what might happen, no teaching to direct them, no tradition to confine them, and no bias or prejudice to restrict them. The experience of the 120 was spontaneous and unadulterated. It was not calculated or planned. The simple fact is, "They were all filled with the Holy Ghost and began to speak with other tongues, as the Spirit gave them utterance" (Acts 2:4). A more exacting precedent will never be found, nor can the honest inquirer err by allowing his faith to be governed by this guideline. The precedent simply reveals that, upon being baptized in the Holy Spirit, men do speak with tongues.

Second is the reason of plurality. In each case where the record is clear, they *all* spoke with tongues. The entire group, present in the upper room on Pentecost, spoke with tongues. The experience was not limited to the apostles, nor to merely the men present, but "they were all filled," including apostles, men, women, laymen.

The same was the case at Cornelius' house. "While Peter yet spake these words, the Holy Ghost fell on all them which heard the word. . . . For they heard them speak with tongues, and magnify God" (Acts 10:44, 46).

And there is little room to doubt that all spoke with tongues when the Ephesian believers were baptized in the Spirit. "And when Paul had laid his hands upon them, the Holy Ghost came on them; and they spake with tongues, and prophesied. And all the men were about twelve" (Acts 19:6-7).

There is not the slightest hint of support for the "with or without" view.

Third is the reason of pattern. It seems completely reasonable that if a pattern for being baptized in the Holy Spirit is to be sought, there could be no source comparable to the Acts. Therein is an accurate accounting of how the experience occurred repeatedly in the beginning church.

If one were to place the inspired accounts of the five experiences in Acts alongside each other, he would readily see the emergence of a convincing pattern. That pattern would testify unequivocally that whenever men are baptized in the Spirit there is an outward supernatural manifestation which always is speaking in tongues and which may also include magnifying of the Lord and prophesying.

Therefore we conclude, with much assurance, that when men are baptized in the Holy Spirit they speak with other tongues.

There is no basis for believing the experience is received by faith without outward evidence, for true faith always yields biblical evidence of itself.

Likewise, the "with or without" theory most assuredly misses the mark of biblical truth.

The preponderance of evidence cries aloud, "Tongues is the initial, physical evidence of the baptism in the Holy Spirit!"

Why Not Wind and Fire?

Early in my ministry I was plagued with a theological question for which I could not find a totally satisfactory answer. Study and pondering seemed to produce no solution.

Then one day as I sat in my study, like a flash from another world, I suddenly discovered the answer which has completely satisfied me from that day to this. I give all glory to God, for I am confident He led me to the truth by His Holy Spirit.

Here is the question: Why do the Pentecostals, who make such a case for tongues speaking as the initial physical evidence of the baptism in the Holy Spirit, almost completely overlook the other two supernatural signs which occurred when the Holy Spirit was first outpoured? Why insist upon tongues speaking, yet pass over the "sound . . . as of a rushing mighty wind" and the appearance of "tongues like as of fire" almost as though they had no part in the momentous event (Acts 2:2-3)?

In his book *What About Tongues Speaking?* Anthony Hoekema puts it this way: "What the 120 received on Pentecost Day, therefore, were three miraculous signs to assure them that the promised outpouring of the Spirit had really occurred. Tongues speaking was only one of these signs. When Pentecostals contend that the experience of the disciples at Pentecost is a pattern for all believers today, why do they think only of glossalalia and not of the sound of the wind and the fiery tongues?"[6]

We could appeal solely to the biblical account for an answer and do no violence to the truth. Even a cursory examination of every account of the Holy Spirit's outpouring recorded in the Acts will readily reveal that the sound of the rushing mighty wind and the appearance of cloven tongues like as of fire occurred only once, while the speaking with tongues was often repeated. This is noteworthy and indicative. However, while it underscores the singularity of the wind-and-fire phenomenon, and also projects the repetition and continuation of the tongues speaking, it does not explain the reason.

Nevertheless, there is a reason.

Fundamental to our correct understanding is recognition of the fact that on Pentecost two specific things happened: (1) the gift of the Holy Ghost was given, and (2) the Holy Ghost who was now given was received. And there is a vital difference. To comprehend this difference is to be well on the way to a sound and credible answer.

The first momentous and monumental event of the day of Pentecost was the giving of the Holy Spirit as a "gift" over and above the new birth.

There was a specific time in history when the Holy Ghost was given for a special function in the Church age. Likewise there was also a time when He was "not yet given." John is our authority for this, for he says, "In the last day, that great day of the feast, Jesus stood and cried saying, If any man thirst, let him come unto me, and drink. He that believeth on me, as the scripture hath said, out of his belly shall flow rivers of living water. (But this spake he of the Spirit, which they that believe on him should receive: for the Holy Ghost was not yet given:

because that Jesus was not yet glorified.)" (John 7:37-39).

The unmistakable observation of the beloved Apostle was that the Holy Ghost would not be given until Jesus had returned to His glorified state. Jesus himself also indicated this at a later moment: "Nevertheless I tell you the truth; It is expedient for you that I go away: for if I go not away, the Comforter will not come unto you; but if I depart I will send him unto you" (John 16:7).

Peter's sermon on the day of Pentecost is beautifully relevant at this juncture, for he connects what happened in the upper room to the glorification of Jesus in this manner, "Therefore being by the right hand of God exalted, [that is, glorified and seated at His own right hand] and having received of the Father the promise of the Holy Ghost, he hath shed forth this which ye now see and hear" (Acts 2:33).

More will be said later about the promise of the Father alluded to by Peter, but suffice it to say here, on the day of Pentecost, Jesus, the federal head of the Church, having ascended to the Father, and having received of the Father, for His Church, the promised Holy Spirit, gave Him to the Church on that significant day.

How do we know the Holy Spirit was given? The Scriptures assert it and this should suffice.

But how did the 120 know? They had a clear directive from the Lord to wait in Jerusalem until He was given: "And, behold, I send the promise of my Father upon you: but tarry ye in the city of Jerusalem, until ye be endued with power from on high" (Luke 24:49). "For John truly baptized with water; but ye shall be baptized with the Holy Ghost not many days hence" (Acts 1:5).

By what means could they know that He who had been promised had really been given? Was it simply a matter of receiving by faith without any sign or confirming evidence, or was there to be some infallible proof He had come?

Let it be remembered, the 120 were all Jewish, or at least proselytes to Judaism.

To every Jewish mind there were at least three unmistakable symbols of the Holy Spirit—wind, fire, and oil. It is most compatible then with the Jewish perception that God, when He would indicate the Holy Spirit was given, should employ two significant symbols of the Holy Spirit—wind and fire. "And suddenly there came a sound from heaven as of a rushing mighty wind, and it filled all the house where they were sitting. And there appeared unto them cloven tongues like as of fire, and it sat upon each of them" (Acts 2:2-3).

Surely there was not a doubter among them, for they had a twofold witness to demonstrate the fulfillment of their expectancy. In the Jewish economy the burden of proof was assigned to a minimum of two witnesses. ". . . at the mouth of two witnesses, or at the mouth of three witnesses, shall the matter be established" (Deut. 19:15).

Yet another problem remains. Why are these signs not repeated? Why do the charismatics have the speaking with tongues, but seldom if ever similar manifestations of wind and fire? The questions are legitimate, and they have plagued some honest inquirers. But there are answers.

As stated previously, there was a time in history when the Holy Ghost was "not given." The key word is "given."

There is a difference between "being given," which indicates a continuous act, and "given," which indicates a finished act. The point being that when the Head of the Church gave the Holy Spirit on the day of Pentecost, He

gave Him to the Church on a once-for-all b[
glorious fact is, He is given! Even as the atoning
Christ was fraught with absolute finality, a[
need be repeated, so the Holy Ghost was give
being no further need of His being given over
again. He is on hand and available.

Getting back then to the matter of precedent,
be noted that a once-for-all, never-to-be-repe
sets no precedent. If there is possibility of an [
repeated, there is the commensurate possibili[
first act being precedential. But where the poss[
repetition is nonexistent, the need for prec
eliminated. There is now no need of the wind an
the Holy Ghost has been given.

The second thing which happened on the
Pentecost was the receiving of the baptism in [
Spirit.

In a previous chapter we have shown that fait[
the level of knowledge. Here is a meaningful [
By the wind and fire the 120 *knew* the Holy G[
given. Once this knowledge reached them, fai
laid hold and they received Him who was given

Thereafter, in the Acts, the emphasis relatin
baptism in the Spirit is almost totally on receiv
upon the conditions related to receiving.

Consider, for example, the Samaritan exp
Philip's ministry had produced a host of conve
had been baptized in water. The news of it
reached Jerusalem, the apostles sent two of their
Peter and John, to witness what was happenin
share in the ministry there.

Upon arriving, Peter and John learned "t[
Ghost . . . was fallen upon none of them: only th
baptized in the name of the Lord Jesus" (Act 8

37

Wherefore they, "when they were come down, prayed for them, that they might receive the Holy Ghost" (Acts 8:15).

It is not without significance that the prayer did not petition God to give the Holy Ghost. God had already given Him. Why ask God to do what had already been done? Therefore, the prayer of the apostles was not at all concerned with obtaining action on God's part, except as such action might directly aid men to receive the Holy Spirit whom God had made available to them.

There is a beautiful parallel in the gift of salvation. At Calvary, salvation was provided for the whole world on a once-for-all basis. "For in that he died, he died unto sin once" (that is, once for all—Rom. 6:10). The atonement for sin was a full and complete and final act of God on behalf of man and his salvation. God could do no more than bring pressure to bear upon the will of man so he would of his own free will, and by faith, choose to receive the abundant provision of God.

God makes His gracious gifts available to all but forces them upon none. He has made salvation available to all, but only those who receive benefit. He has given the Holy Spirit, but again only those who receive benefit.

Now we have seen that there was no precedent involved in the once-for-all giving of the Holy Spirit. But in the receiving of the Holy Spirit there was most certainly a precedent involved, since what happened at that point was to be repeated throughout the Church age.

It was after the mighty Pentecostal outpouring in the upper room that Peter, speaking by the Spirit, extended the possibility of receiving even to those who at that time were afar off. "Then Peter said unto them, Repent, and be baptized every one of you in the name of Jesus

Christ, for the remission of sins, and ye shall receive the gift of the Holy Ghost. For the promise is unto you, and to your children, and to all that are afar off, even as many as the Lord our God shall call" (Acts 2:38-39).

The precedent for receiving, showing in clearly understandable terms what can be expected to happen in all subsequent instances, is stated in Acts 2:4. "And they were all filled with the Holy Ghost, and began to speak with other tongues, as the Spirit gave them utterance."

It is most difficult to argue with precedent. But why argue with it? Let it rather be God's guiding light to a life filled with His Spirit.

Friend, if you have not yet received according to the precedent, there is something beautiful waiting to happen to you!

In summary:

WHY NOT WIND AND FIRE?

On the day of Pentecost *two* important events occurred.

I. **THE HOLY SPIRIT WAS GIVEN**
   A. The evidence
      1. Wind
      2. Fire
   B. The precedent
      Non-precedential, because the Holy Spirit was given on a once-for-all basis.

II. **THE HOLY SPIRIT, WHO WAS GIVEN, WAS RECEIVED**
   A. The evidence
      Speaking in unknown tongues
   B. The precedent
      Precedential, because the Holy Spirit is to be received by believers throughout the Church age.

five

Tongues Are Good for You

Blanche Britton Urdahl was an unusually effective evangelist in the earlier days of the modern Pentecostal movement. She blazed a trail of evangelism across the upper Midwest, and several churches exist today as the fruit of her labors. Though she departed this life many years ago, she lives on in the lives of many who came under the powerful impact of her God-anointed ministry. Among these is the Rev. G. Raymond Carlson, assistant general superintendent of the Assemblies of God.

In the early 1940s, Mrs. Urdahl (then Mrs. Britton) was conducting a series of evangelistic services in the church I was then pastoring in western North Dakota.

Attending those services was the county judge's wife, who had been the wife of an evangelical minister for forty years until his decease. She was a godly woman and loved the spirit she sensed in our services. But she was quite adamantly non-Pentecostal. Yet strangely enough she dearly loved the evangelist.

On a certain night Evangelist Britton spoke about the Holy Spirit and speaking in other tongues. I well remember that after the service had ended these two ladies stood talking to each other. The judge's wife said to the evangelist, "But I don't want to speak with tongues."

And I will never forget Mrs. Britton's answer. Very kindly, but very wisely, she replied, "Well, sister, don't worry. You never will speak with tongues if you don't want to."

And that is the truth. No one has to speak with tongues. Nevertheless, I hasten to add, there is great advantage to be derived from it.

I am persuaded that Satan delights in robbing people of what God has provided to be a tremendous plusfactor in their spiritual lives.

Of the nine gifts enumerated in 1 Cor. 12:8-10, to only one is attributed force for personal edification. "He that speaketh in an unknown tongue edifieth himself" (1 Cor. 14:4).

Then Paul adds, "I would that you all spake with tongues" (1 Cor. 14:5) and, "I thank my God, I speak with tongues more than ye all" (1 Cor. 14:18).

Surely there is no greater authority on this subject than Paul. He could not be accused of being a theorist. His teaching sprang from his personal experience in the school of the Spirit. And the Spirit directed him in his instructions to the Corinthians.

The Greek word *oikodomē* employed by Paul and translated "edify" or "edification," means to build or to be built up. Applying this to the spiritual man, it carries the idea of spiritual growth and development.

How beautiful! The man who gives evidence of greatest spiritual growth and development is the very man who testified, "I speak with tongues more than ye all." Therein is a lesson for all of us.

Concerning Paul's early Christian walk, Luke records, "But Saul increased the more in strength, and confounded the Jews which dwelt at Damascus, proving that this is the very Christ" (Acts 9:22).

"Increased the more in strength" is translated from the Greek *endunamoō*, which means to strengthen or put power in. And the implication here is to be strengthened or empowered with supernatural power, to be built up spiritually. Could it be that Paul learned very early in his Spirit-filled life this beautiful and valuable function of the gift of tongues?

Jude also has a word of exhortation regarding the edifying of ourselves. He writes, "But ye, beloved, building up yourselves on your most holy faith, praying in the Holy Ghost" (v. 20). It follows then that praying in the Holy Ghost is praying in tongues, for Paul wrote, "I will pray with the spirit" (1 Cor. 14:15).

There is a further consideration with regard to tongues for personal edification.

Tongues speaking is not limited to prayer. It is also a beautiful device for praise. Charles Wesley wrote, "O for a thousand tongues to sing my great Redeemer's praise." We wonder if he discovered the gift of tongues by which this could be possible.

While prayer is usually geared to getting, praise is usually geared to giving. And it is through giving of praise through the unknown tongue that our spirits ascend to the highest heights.

"Praise is comely," wrote the Psalmist (Ps. 33:1), and ". . . thou art holy, O thou that inhabitest the praises of Israel" (Ps. 22:3).

When the Holy Spirit fell upon Cornelius and his household, "they heard them speak with tongues and magnify God" (Acts 10:45). It seems quite clear the tongues speaking and the magnifying of God were not two separate things. Rather, the tongues speaking was the means of the magnification.

I have seen it scores of times and have experienced it myself. The newly filled-with-the-Spirit individual discovers a means of praise beyond anything he has ever known. Like a gushing torrent the worship of the Father and the Son bursts forth.

Let the honest doubter stand by when a believer receives a mighty baptism. He will witness praise and worship unparalleled in any other experience. And the speaker himself will rise up from that initial experience built up to a new stature never known before.

An observation should be noted here. Some have attributed tongues speaking to the devil. Paul shared a bit of spiritual wisdom with the Corinthians when he wrote, "Wherefore I give you to understand, that no man speaking by the Spirit of God calleth Jesus accursed: and that no man can say Jesus is Lord, but by the Holy Ghost" (1 Cor. 12:3).

He is clearly talking of men speaking by the Spirit, or under the sway of the Spirit, and he states the absolute conviction that when this is the case, the Lordship of Jesus will be declared and there will be no calling of Jesus accursed. And thus it is. In all of the experiences I have witnessed, I have yet to hear anyone speaking in the Spirit and calling Jesus accursed. Always Jesus is extolled and exalted and worshiped for the God who He truly is. This in itself is a most convincing evidence of the genuineness of the experience.

Nor should the tongues speaking cease thereafter. It should be the daily means of spiritual strengthening and upbuilding. Multiplied thousands have found it so, and they will unashamedly testify that tongues speaking is good for them.

For the further encouragement of the honest inquirer I share the following testimonies from charismatic leaders of stature in the present hour.

Father Dennis Bennett, former rector of St. Luke's Episcopal Church in Seattle, has this to say: "So many times, after praying, I had stopped with the feeling that there was so much more to be said, but I just didn't have the words. One great value of this strange phenomenon of 'speaking in tongues' I discovered . . . was that I could pray beyond the limitations of the intellect, telling God the things that needed to be expressed, but for which I had no words.

". . . something else began to happen. My heart began to get happier and happier! The Presence of God that I had so clearly seen in earlier days to be the real reason for living suddenly enveloped me again after many, many years of dryness. Never had I experienced God's presence in such reality as now. It might have frightened me, except that I recognized that this was the same Presence of the Lord that I had sensed when I first accepted Jesus . . . only the intensity and reality of my present experience was far greater than anything I had believed possible. If those earlier experiences were like flashbulbs, this was as if someone had suddenly turned on the floodlights."[7]

Nearly seventy years ago, Ernest S. Williams was baptized in the Spirit. Later he became one of the stalwarts of the Assemblies of God and served that movement for twenty years as its general superintendent. Although he is not far from becoming a centenarian, he still has an effective and useful ministry. He recently shared this testimony with me: "I was saved from the condemnation of sin November 13, 1904. I received a gracious infilling with the Spirit, accompanied with speaking in other tongues, October 2, 1905.

"I have never felt impressed to speak in tongues in public services, but speaking in tongues has ever been, and still is, a most enriching experience, when it wells up from within in my private devotions when waiting and worshiping.

"I greatly appreciate this spiritual manifestation, but have never worshiped the gift, or other spiritual gifts. The center of my worship has ever been the Lord Jesus Christ, my Savior and Lord, greatly enriched through the quickening blessing of speaking in other tongues in holy communion with the Father, and His Son, our Lord Jesus Christ."

Add to these the meaningful affidavit of Thomas F. Zimmerman, internationally known charismatic leader and present general superintendent of the Assemblies of God: "The joyous experience of speaking in other tongues has been a tremendous dimension of spiritual blessing and edification in my personal life. This benefit has been most meaningful in the area of intercessory prayer as I am led by the Spirit to intercede at times in a language which I have never learned. This, of course, is in fulfillment of that which the Apostle Paul implies when he speaks of 'praying in the Spirit.' It also fulfills the further reference to praying with 'groanings' which do not find adequate expression in the language known unto man. It has been my joyous experience to pray in an unknown tongue with a conscious anointing of the Holy Spirit.

"Further edification has come to me in times when, through the Spirit's utterance, I have been lifted to a plane of meaningful worship where I have been able to express an innermost ecstasy of spirit and soul in worship to God over and beyond that which is available through just a mere human tongue. It is indeed a great blessing of soul to be able to worship God either in speaking with other tongues or in the joy of singing in the Spirit, as a very meaningful personal relationship with God is achieved through this type of spiritual worship.

"I have not looked upon the matter of speaking in other tongues as being an unimportant adjunct of New Testament worship and prayer. In my opinion it is the provision of God for the New Testament church to be able to effectively pray and worship at a level and in a dimension beyond that which can be humanly understood and articulated."

Finally, I share with you the testimony of G. Raymond Carlson, assistant general superintendent of the Assemblies of God.

"God has given us an intimate secret language of prayer for our personal edification. Scarcely a day passes but what, by the Holy Spirit, I employ this sacred experience.

"In preparation for pulpit ministry, I have found that speaking in tongues in personal prayer and praise is one of the most profitable ways of readying myself for ministry in the Holy Spirit. The same obtains when preparing for a time of counseling or decision making.

"Another great value is the relaxation of tension— 'rest and refreshing'—as the burdens of life press upon me. I have found that the Spirit helps my prayer life and prays through me with a feeling that cannot be expressed. Spiritual therapy takes place. There is a sense of praying with the mind of the Spirit in the will of God and of the very real presence of Christ.

"As a boy of ten I was baptized in the Holy Spirit. During the years God has permitted me to give utterances in tongues and/or interpretation of tongues in public services. Yet the greatest source of edification to me has been those hours of deep devotion as day by day in mutual unity with the abiding Comforter I prayed and worshiped in other tongues, and quite often silently in the midst of the throbbing noise of people around me."

Thus we arrive at the inspiring conclusion that tongues are good for you.

six

Are We Missing Something?

"Tongues plus interpretation equals prophecy." This is apparently the most commonly accepted view among Pentecostals. Notwithstanding, there is another view which is worthy of in-depth consideration.

We should remind ourselves at this point that faith is governed by knowledge. And whether knowledge is perfect or not, faith operates within the framework of that knowledge and can rarely, if ever, transcend it.

Therefore it is of utmost importance that accurate knowledge be pursued with diligence.

Knowledge is more often than not the fruit of experience. Yet experience is not always a teacher of truth. To restrict knowledge to the boundaries determined by experience is to place a straitjacket on truth.

The Scriptures themselves are the repository of absolute truth. "Thy word is true," wrote the Psalmist (Ps. 119:160), and Jesus supported the same idea when He said, "thy word is truth" (John 17:17). Unless we accept the Word as the supreme court in our quest for knowledge, we will most likely wander far afield.

It is not easy for any of us to admit we may come short of knowledge and truth. Yet it is only when we reach this difficult pinnacle of admitting our possible shortcomings that we are in a place where truth may bestow upon us her richest treasures.

Tradition and experience and even an on-the-surface

interpretation of Scripture have united to give us the knowledge that governs our manifestation of the gift of tongues. They have taught us that tongues when interpreted obtain the same end as does the single gift of prophecy—edification, exhortation and comfort—and that through this means God chooses to speak to His children.

It has been thus concluded that through both the single gift of prophecy and the two gifts of tongues and interpretation God speaks to His people. In consequence of this conclusion, a framework of knowledge has emerged, and faith, operating within that framework, has yielded either a prophetic utterance or what is commonly known as a message in tongues and an interpretation. And in each case the utterance is directed toward men.

Nevertheless, as the Scriptures dealing with this matter are carefully examined, the searcher for truth is confronted with some questions which deserve honest attention. Is tongues, when interpreted, the same in content and purpose as prophecy? Are these gifts, as they operate, always in the form of an utterance directed to those present? Is there, after all, such a thing as a "message in tongues"? Might we have overlooked some important truth which could bless the Church?

To set the stage for our quest for truth we resort to Paul's statements which seem to indicate the direction of the two gifts of tongues and prophecy: "For he that speaketh in an unknown tongue speaketh not unto men, but unto God . . . he that prophesieth speaketh unto men" (1 Cor. 14:2-3). Taking these two statements at face value, there is an unavoidable implication that speaking with tongues is always directed toward God, and that prophecy is always directed toward man. Is it possible that this is true and that we have missed some-

50

thing of importance relating to the gift of tongues?

The only sound and dependable answer will come from an objective examination of biblical evidence. Therefore we will give attention to each recorded instance of tongues speaking, as well as to Paul's comments on the subject.

First consider the tongues speaking on the day of Pentecost. "And they were all filled with the Holy Ghost, and began to speak with other tongues, as the Spirit gave them utterance. And there were dwelling at Jerusalem Jews, devout men, out of every nation under heaven. Now when this was noised abroad, the multitude came together, and were confounded, because that every man heard them speak in his own language. And they were all amazed and marvelled, saying one to another, Behold, are not all these which speak Galileans? And how hear we every man in our own tongue, wherein we were born? Parthians, and Medes, and Elamites, and the dwellers in Mesopotamia, and in Judaea, and Cappadocia, in Pontus, and Asia, Phrygia, and Pamphylia, in Egypt, and in the parts of Libya about Cyrene, and strangers of Rome, Jews and proselytes, Cretes and Arabians, we do hear them speak in our tongues the wonderful works of God" (Acts 2:4-11).

To whom was that original tongues speaking addressed? Surely those speaking were not addressing each other. What folly it would have been for them to speak to their fellows in tongues unknown to themselves, and not understood by those who heard.

Nor were they preaching in tongues to the outside crowd, for when the tongues speaking began, the crowd had not yet assembled. It was only after the news got out that the crowd gathered. "Now when this was noised abroad, the multitude came together . . ." (Acts 2:6).

Some have construed that, once the crowd gathered, the gospel was preached to them through supernatural tongues speaking. There is not a shred of evidence to support the idea. The fact is that the tongues speaking which had started before the crowd arrived simply continued on. But the onlookers understood what they were saying. And when they inquired as to what the strange phenomenon meant, Peter preached the gospel to them in a tongue common to himself and to all of them.

Now, since the tongues speakers certainly were not addressing each other, and since they also certainly were not addressing the crowd, which had not arrived, the reasonable conclusion is that in their tongues speaking they were addressing God as they spoke of "the wonderful works of God" (Acts 2:11). "For he that speaketh in an unknown tongue speaketh not unto men, but unto God" (1 Cor. 14:2).

Tongues speaking is mentioned again in Acts 10:44-46. "While Peter yet spake these words, the Holy Ghost fell on all them which heard the word. And they of the circumcision which believed were astonished, as many as came with Peter, because that on the Gentiles also was poured out the gift of the Holy Ghost. For they heard them speak with tongues, and magnify God."

To whom did Cornelius and his household address their tongues speaking? Again there is no slight hint that they spoke to each other, for as at Pentecost, that would have made no sense.

Did they address Peter and his companions? That is extremely doubtful.

To whom then did they speak? Quite obviously, God. "For they heard them speak with tongues, and magnify God" (Acts 10:46). A better translation might read, "For they heard them speak with tongues, magnifying God."

Another account of tongues speaking is in Acts 19:6. "And when Paul had laid his hands upon them, the Holy Ghost came on them; and they spake with tongues, and prophesied."

As in the two previous cases, it makes little sense to believe that the tongues speakers addressed each other in their new unknown tongues, or even that they addressed Paul. Nay, rather, as always, the tongues speaking was unto God.

The next reference to tongues speaking whence we might gain a further sense of direction is 1 Cor. 14:2. "For he that speaketh in an unknown tongue speaketh not unto men, but unto God: for no man understandeth him; howbeit in the spirit he speaketh mysteries."

Traditionally it is conceived that here Paul is speaking of the personal edification aspect of tongues speaking and not of that function of the gift for edification of the body. But this view is hardly compatible with sound hermeneutics. To attempt to resolve the problem by delineating between tongues as a gift and tongues of another sort is to cloud the issue unfairly. If the references to prophecy in 1 Cor. 14:1 and 3 are references to the gift of prophecy, by what rule can we safely conclude that the tongues reference of 1 Cor. 14:2 is not a reference to the gift of tongues?

It is my view, as indicated in a previous chapter, that there is but a single gift of tongues which encompasses several facets of manifestation, and that in all of these facets of manifestation, Paul's declaration, "For he that speaketh in an unknown tongue speaketh not unto men but unto God" applies.

When such a view is held, other problems must be faced. What of 1 Cor. 14:5? "I would that ye all spake with tongues, but rather that ye prophesied: for greater is he that prophesieth than he that speaketh with tongues, except he interpret, that the church may receive edifying."

On the basis of Paul's statement, ". . . greater is he that prophesieth than he that speaketh with tongues, except he interpret" (1 Cor. 14:5), it has been concluded that tongues plus interpretation is equal to prophecy. Thus, since the prophetic utterance which is for the express purpose of "edification, exhortation, and comfort" is obviously directed toward the church, the logical conclusion is that tongues which are interpreted are a message to the church; and in consequence, we have the expression "message in tongues." It follows then that if interpretation is directed churchward the utterance being interpreted is also directed churchward.

The traditional view:

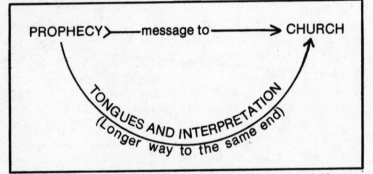

PROPHECY⟩——message to——→ CHURCH

TONGUES AND INTERPRETATION
(Longer way to the same end)

Nevertheless, let us examine a somewhat different point of view. Attention must be given to Paul's central concern—the edification of the church through proper manifestation of the gifts. There is little to support the idea that tongues interpreted is equal to prophecy in content. The degree of greatness to which Paul alludes (1 Cor. 14:5) in his projection of comparisons is in respect to force for edification. What he is saying is that the prophet, by his utterance, is more of a force for edification than is the speaker with tongues, except the latter interprets. He is hardly contradicting his former statement that "he that speaketh in an unknown tongue speaketh not unto men, but unto God." Nor does he in any way indicate that interpretation of tongues changes the direction of the original utterance. If the speaking in tongues follows what Paul said about it—that it is addressed to God and not to men—then the interpretation of it should be addressed to God, not to men. There is good reason for this as we shall see later.

It is just here that I wonder if we are not missing something which God intends for His Church to enjoy, and by which her members can gain spiritual profit. By the traditional view that tongues plus interpretation equals prophecy, is it not being said that tongues and interpretation are the long way around to the same end gained by the single means of prophecy?

But if tongues speaking is always directed Godward, it changes the picture distinctly. How? Just this way. It gives tongues speaking in the church a function all of its own. Instead of being in the form of a message directed toward the church, which is always the case with prophecy, it is intended to be a form of worship and prayer. This worship and prayer interpreted generates participation on the part of other members of the body, and thus it becomes a means of edification equal to prophecy. In prophecy the edification springs from the Spirit-quickened Word, while in tongues and interpretation the edification springs from Spirit-quickened worship and prayer.

Spirit-quickened worship and prayer is the cure for a thousand ills, and the means to spiritual higher ground. Are we coming short of this by our failure to recognize the divine intent for tongues and interpretation?

An objection to the view that tongues speaking is always directed toward God is sometimes raised on the basis of 1 Cor. 14:6, "Now brethren, if I come unto you

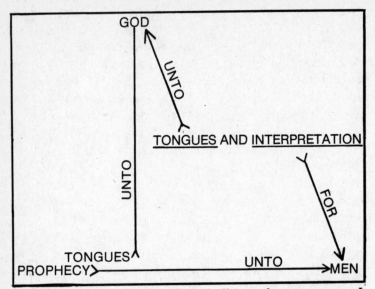

speaking with tongues, what shall I profit you, except I shall speak to you either by revelation, or by knowledge, or by prophesying, or by doctrine?" It is held that here Paul is projecting the content of interpretation of tongues, and is thus indicating that tongues may be directed toward men.

However, this may be an inaccurate conclusion. We must not be forgetful that Paul is concerned with excessive uses of the tongues gift which would militate against the edification of the church. His obvious point is that though speaking with tongues is of value for edification, if kept within proper bounds, there is much profiting missed unless room is given for other ministry—revelation, knowledge, prophecy, doctrine.

Other Scripture attests to this view. "How is it then, brethren? when ye come together, every one hath a doctrine, hath a tongue, hath a revelation, hath an interpretation" (1 Cor. 14:26). If interpretation of tongues might include setting forth a doctrine or a revelation, from the writer's point of view it would be somewhat superfluous to have a list like this. It seems clear that "doctrine" and "revelation" are distinct from "tongues" and "interpretation," and are therefore listed along with them. Thus we may well conclude that in verse 6 Paul is not mindful of the content of tongues, but rather he is seeking to underline the importance of making room for ministry other than tongues speaking, which apparently was dominant in the Corinthian gatherings.

Another objection may be raised to the idea that tongues is always directed toward God on the basis of 1 Cor. 14:21 where Paul writes, "In the law it is written, With men of other tongues and other lips will I speak unto this people. . . ." It would not be difficult to conclude from this statement that, at least in some instances, the gift of tongues is intended to bring a message from God to men—that is, that through this gift God does address himself to men. Nevertheless, let us look more closely at the passage.

What is God really saying? Is He indicating that by the gift of tongues He would convey the gospel to Israel, that He would aim a message toward them through messengers, who not knowing their language would address themselves to Israel in their own tongue? Or is He rather saying that the appearance of the tongues gift, whereby men would speak languages unknown to themselves but known to Israel, would in itself be God's means of speaking to Israel? If the latter is the case, the direction toward which the utterance is aimed is not the concern, but it is rather the fact of the phenomenon. In other words, God would speak to Israel, not necessarily in a direct message to them, but by permitting an easily recognizable supernatural manifestation, through which, if they would, they could discern divine reality.

How shall we know? Without doubt we will come nearest to the correct answer by examining the biblical record of the prophecy's fulfillment as given in Acts 2.

When the day of Pentecost came and the 120 began speaking with tongues, the record simply states, "we do hear them speak in our tongues the wonderful works of God" (Acts 2:11). The evidence points to the fact that it was not necessarily what was said, or even to whom it was addressed, that captivated the hearers. It was rather that Galileans were observed speaking languages not understood by themselves, but understood by an impressive list of Jewish foreigners who were on hand for the Feast of Pentecost. "And they were all amazed and marvelled, saying one to another, Behold, are not all these which speak Galileans? And how hear we every man in our own tongue, wherein we were born?" (Acts 2:7-8). Through this phenomenon God spoke to the gathered multitude, and thus the gift of tongues became "a sign, not to them that believe, but to them that believe not" (1 Cor. 14:22).

There is yet more evidence to support the idea that tongues speaking is, upon every manifestation, directed toward God. In his continuing discussion of the gift of tongues, Paul says, "For if I pray in an unknown tongue, my spirit prayeth . . ." (1 Cor. 14:14). And again he says, "I will pray with the spirit" and, "I will sing with the spirit . . ." (1 Cor. 14:15). All will agree that prayer, whether in the spirit, that is, in tongues, and even ordinary prayer for that matter, is toward God, and not toward men. Furthermore, singing in the spirit is also unto God according to the context.

A careful examination of the context relating to these matters is extremely enlightening.

Begin at 1 Cor. 14:12. "Even so ye, forasmuch as ye are zealous of spiritual gifts, seek that ye may excel to the edifying of the church." That is a straightforward directive concerning motives for manifestation of the gifts. The motive must be to excel to edify. Anything less is unworthy employment of the gifts.

The "wherefore" of verse 13 unmistakably ties it to verse 12. Dr. Paul Rees, a widely known evangelical, has stated that when you see a "therefore" in the Scriptures, you ought to find out what it is there for. The same rule applies to the "wherefores" of Scripture.

"Wherefore," that is, since edification is the objective, "let him that speaketh in an unknown tongue pray that he may interpret." The point is that tongues apart from interpretation does not edify the Body, because the Body has no way of knowing the mysteries He is speaking. Only as the tongue is interpreted can the body benefit.

The Pulpit Commentary has a noteworthy rendering of verse 3. "So pray as to be able to interpret, or pray with the object of afterwards interpreting."[8]

If this is an accurate translation, the function of the gift of interpretation is related to praying in tongues, which means then that tongues speaking in the church may be in the form of a prayer, and that when this is the case, interpretation is required.

Moving on to verse 14, Paul, yet speaking about the importance of interpreting what has been prayed in a tongue, explains, "For if I pray in an unknown tongue, my spirit prayeth, but [apart from the gift of interpretation] my understanding is unfruitful."

Then comes the question: "What is it then?" (verse 15). That is, what shall I, as one who prays in a tongue in the church, do? Another question should be asked at this juncture: Is there anything in Scripture indicating that tongues speaking ever takes any other form than prayer and singing unto God? It is extremely doubtful.

Now Paul answers his own question. "I will pray with the spirit" (that is, in tongues) and "I will pray with the understanding also." Does he mean, as we have for so long thought, that he would pray supernaturally in tongues, and that he would also pray from his own mind on the natural plane? No way! He plainly, in light of his previous instruction relating to the gift of interpretation, says, "I will pray in tongues, and then I will interpret what I have prayed."

The exact same practice would apply to his singing with the spirit. "I will sing with the spirit, and I will interpret what I sing."

Verse 16 sets the seal to all of this, and adds some beautiful new light. There Paul says, "Else," that is, "otherwise," the idea being that if you fail to follow these guidelines requiring you to interpret in the public meeting what you have prayed or sung in a tongue, how shall those who can't understand what you are saying say "Amen" and be edified? ". . . when thou shalt bless with the spirit, how shall he that occupieth the room of the unlearned say Amen at thy giving of thanks, seeing he understandeth not what thou sayest? For thou verily givest thanks well, but the other is not edified" (1 Cor. 14:16-17).

Here we are introduced to a clearer understanding of what praying and singing in tongues encompasses—*blessing God* and *giving thanks unto God*. In other words, tongues is the worship gift for the edifying of the church. Therefore, when one blesses God and gives thanks in a tongue, and then follows his tongues speaking with the interpretation, the whole body is edified because they can say, "Amen at thy giving of thanks."

"The custom of ratifying prayer and praises with the 'Amen' of hearty assent and participation existed in the Jewish as well as in the Christian church. The sound of the loud unanimous 'Amen' of early Christian congregations is compared to the echo of distant thunder.

"Being the answer of the congregation, the 'Amen' was regarded as no less important than the prayer itself" (*The Pulpit Commentary*).[9]

Thus we conclude that Scripture, relating to tongues speaking, is constant and consistent in setting forth the idea that "He that speaketh in an unknown tongue speaketh not unto men, but unto God" (1 Cor. 14:2).

Now, I freely acknowledge that the position set forth above is not without some problems. For instance, the question naturally surfaces, "If tongues is always directed Godward, how can we explain the fact that experience seems to contradict this?" And what about our "messages in tongues"?

First, I recognize experience must be considered. Certainly we cannot write it off lightly, for in a sense it is the essence of life. Yet most of us are agreed the Scriptures must be revered above experience.

Second, we acknowledge that experience is the fruit of faith, which as we have previously indicated, is governed and circumscribed by knowledge. The relation of knowledge to experience cannot be gainsaid, whether that knowledge is accurate or not.

In this light there are several possible solutions to the problem. Is it possible that what we commonly accept as interpretation of tongues is actually prophecy, and that tongues, rather than being truly interpreted, simply inspire faith for the prophetic utterance?

Furthermore, is it not reasonable to believe that God accommodates himself to the level of understanding and faith? Church history is replete with examples.

Does God stand in judgment if we have been in error? A thousand times no! He delights in every opportunity to manifest himself, though the vessels may not have perfect knowledge. He winks at our ignorance, and, if I may say it, I think He smiles at our folly. But I hasten to add, He greatly desires that we pursue knowledge with a pure heart, so that we, as individuals and the church, may attain the greatest heights.

If we have imperfections, and without doubt we do, it is imperative that we seek greater light lest we miss something which God intends for the church's edification.

A friend of mine purchased a Mercury automobile. After using and enjoying it for three years he decided to sell it.

Desiring that the auto would be in the best possible condition for selling, he took it to a mechanic for a tune-up. While conversing with the mechanic he commented, "This is such a good car. I only wish it had a passing gear."

"It does," replied the mechanic.

"Oh, no, I've driven it for three years and it just doesn't have a passing gear."

Whereupon the mechanic proceeded to make a slight adjustment and sure enough, it had a passing gear!

What was the problem? Why had my friend driven without the benefit of a passing gear for three years? Why did he miss out on something of such importance?

There is only one answer. He just did not know what was available to him all the time.

No doubt it is the same with us. God has provided the wonderful worship gift, the gift of tongues, for edification of the body. But through our ignorance of God's intended purpose for the gift, we have settled for something, to say the least, which is much less than God has planned for the Church to enjoy.

seven

Tongues for the Feebleminded

By comparison with the infinite God, "feebleminded" is too generous a term to express the mental powers of us who are but animated specks of dust.

Let all men admit they do not hold a candle to God. And the sooner the better. Until a man grasps this he has not entered the school of spiritual understanding.

Isaiah the prophet, uttering the words of God, draws back the curtain and exposes our finiteness when he says, "For my thoughts are not your thoughts, neither are your ways my ways, saith the Lord. For as the heavens are higher than the earth, so are my ways higher than your ways, and my thoughts than your thoughts" (Isa. 55:8-9).

And again Isaiah wrote, "To whom then will ye liken God? or what likeness will ye compare unto him?" (Isa. 40:18).

To compare ourselves with other men is folly. "For we dare not make ourselves of the number, or compare ourselves with some that commend themselves: but they measuring themselves, and comparing themselves among themselves, are not wise" (2 Cor. 10:12). It is far more comfortable and greatly to the advantage of our well-being to accept ourselves for who we are and how God made us as individuals. To think more highly of ourselves than we ought to think is to play into the hand of devastating pride. On the other hand, to think less of ourselves than is the truth is to shortchange ourselves and dishonor God.

Let each man be who he is under God, and let him be that man to the full. No more. No less. But, at the same time, let each man perceive his own utter finiteness, for therein is a key to enablement beyond himself.

I remember, when in my earliest pastoral experience, I suddenly became aware of my own finiteness as compared to God's infinity.

Mentally I had plunged into space. I had soared beyond the moon, the sun, the Milky Way, the most distant star. On and on I went in search for an end of the universe, but I could comprehend no end. My mind could not fathom it. Everything I knew had an end. How could a thing have no end? Everything human and everything earthly has an end.

Then I went backward into the eternal past. Back. Back. Back. Back to the advent of Christ. Back to original man. Back to the creation of earth and the universe itself. Yet at each point I knew I had not discovered the beginning of beginnings. Again my mind could not fathom it. All I had known had a point of beginning. But now I was confronted with infinity. And in glimpsing this I saw also my own utter finiteness. That helped me.

Perhaps more than any other New Testament author, Paul was aware of human limitations and feebleness. This came into clear view in his letter to the Romans when he wrote, "Likewise the Spirit also helpeth our infirmities" (Rom. 8:26). "Infirmities" is a translation of the Greek *astheneia,* which means literally feebleness (of mind or body).

Assuredly Paul was in no way indicting the Roman Christians, nor even humans in general. His use of the term was in no sense a comparison of one human with another. Rather he was purposefully drawing a comparison between the mind of man and the mind of the Spirit. With his enlightened understanding he perceived the almost extreme limitation of the mind of man in ascertaining the will of God. When it comes to prayer, and we can be confident he needed look no farther than himself, he says, "we know not what we should pray for as we ought" (Rom. 8:26).

Who of us has not felt the depths of his own inadequacy when he has prayed? Surely the man who has not confronted this has scarcely prayed. He who has prayed most will likely be first to acknowledge his own "feeblemindedness" when it comes to praying according to the will of God.

Howbeit, this is not a problem without an answer. For Paul says, "The Spirit . . . helpeth our infirmities [feeblemindedness]." What a glorious truth!

"Helpeth" derives from the Greek *sunantilambanomai*, which means "to take hold of opposite together, i.e., cooperate (assist)—help" (Strong). I get the idea of a tug of war. Many of us have childhood memories of choosing sides for such an event. A knot was tied at the halfway point in a long rope. Then a line was drawn on the ground, to be directly below the knot when the game began. The object was to overbalance the opposite side by exercising enough pull to force them across the line. Sometimes the sides were so evenly matched that neither side could outpull the other. And sometimes a strong person would join one side, thus completely pulling the other side off balance.

Thus it is too in our spiritual conflicts. Sometimes we find ourselves in a mental and spiritual war. The forces of evil tug against us and we find ourselves too feeble to triumph. But then the Holy Spirit comes to our aid and tugs with us, thus enabling us to overpower the enemy and to gain the desired end.

The "feebleminded" have an unlimited resource. Those who know not how to pray as they ought have a Helper who "maketh intercession for the saints according to the will of God" (Rom. 8:27).

Just how does the Spirit do this? Does He carry on this function apart from human agency, or is there some way in which the feeble human is involved? *The Pulpit Commentary* says, "Not as the Son intercedes for them, apart from themselves at the mercy seat; but within themselves, by inspiring them with these unutterable (or, muttered) groanings: and they are conscious that such deep and intense yearnings are from the Divine Spirit moving them, and teaching them to pray."[10] And the text itself indicates the Spirit helps our "feeblemindedness"; that is, He lifts us above the human level to a plane where we are indeed praying in the will of God.

Is Paul alluding to a special quickening of human perception until the will of God is clearly perceived and becomes the ground for our praying? Hardly. For he says, "the Spirit itself [himself] maketh intercession."

In what way does the Spirit intercede? The answer is *with groanings which cannot be uttered.* On this *The Pulpit*

Commentary says, "They may not still be able to put their requests of God into definite form, or even express them in words; but they know that God knows the meaning of what his own Spirit has inspired."[11] But is Paul not saying, "with language beyond human words?" I believe so.

I think Paul had the same idea in focus when he instructed the Ephesians, "Praying always with all prayer and supplication in the Spirit" (Eph. 6:18). And Jude seems to voice the same concept in his directive, "But ye, beloved, building up yourselves on your most holy faith, praying in the Holy Ghost" (Jude 20).

This is where praying in tongues plays a tremendously meaningful role, and, in the same vein wherein tongues is for the "feebleminded," it provides a whole new dimension to prayer. It enables the believer to soar into the heavenlies and to appear beneath the scepter-raised hand of God with utmost confidence that he is praying according to the will of God. "And this is the confidence that we have in him, that, if we ask anything according to his will, he heareth us: And if we know that he hear us, whatever we ask, we know that we have the petitions that we desired of him" (1 John 5:14-15).

Paul himself testified to his own use of this glorious means. To the Corinthians he wrote, "if I pray in an unknown tongue, my spirit prayeth. . . . What is it then? I will pray with the spirit. . ." (1 Cor. 14:14-15).

Writing on this intriguing subject, Harold Horton, a respected British scholar, says, "You cannot pray with the spirit unless you speak with other tongues. . . . You can neither pray nor sing with the spirit unless you speak with tongues. The loose statements of the commentators on these things have the effect, if not the design, of sweeping away the supernatural. Once again it is necessary to warn young Christians against that exegesis that degrades the supernatural in the Bible to the powerless and undistinguished level of the natural. 'We know not what we should pray for as we ought.' The Spirit both knows and is able. 'He maketh intercession for us (and through us) with groanings that cannot be uttered.' How often has a Spirit-filled child of God poured forth his soul in agonizing supplication for he knows not what or whom, to find perhaps a year afterwards an echo of his prayer-in-tongues in the miraculous deliverance of some missionary in peril, or some beloved one a thousand miles away at death's door! Think not that these things have no meaning. Praying in tongues is an exercise more potent in its own mysterious realm than the mightiest praying with the understanding. Let us humbly say that those not filled with the Spirit know nothing of these supernatural things. Not for nought has the all-seeing Lord designed an instrument that will reach in its galvanic range circumstances and situations that are infinitely beyond the sweep of poor creature sense and ability. For 'the Searcher of hearts knows what the Spirit's meaning is, because His intercessions are in harmony with God's will' [Rom. 8:27, Weymouth], whereas our human intercessions according to the understanding so often are not."[12]

How valid is this idea? Does it really work today?

In John Sherrill's book *They Speak With Other Tongues*, he shares this supportive testimony: "One of the most startling instances I know of when the intellect refused to pray in an emergency, was related to me by William C. Nelson. The Reverend Mr. Nelson is now editor of *Frontiers* for the American Baptist Convention, but at the time this incident took place, he was pastor of the First Baptist Church in Whiteman, Massachusetts.

"In the dead of night, one evening in the fall of 1959, the telephone beside Bill's bed rang. Fumbling for the receiver, Bill was still groggy when a woman's voice identified itself as belonging to a nurse at a nearby hospital. There had been an automobile accident, the voice continued.

" 'We have Carol Vinall here. Her mother gave your name as minister. You better get here right away if you're coming. Doctor doesn't think she'll live another hour.'

" 'I'll be there.'

"Bill threw his clothes on and crowded the speed limit every mile of the way in to the hospital. The desk had been alerted that he was coming, and sent him up to the third floor. The clock across from the elevator said 3:15 a.m.

" 'This way,' said the nurse.

"Thirteen-year-old Carol lay in a high-sided bed with no sign of life about her. Her mother stood beside the oxygen tent. 'It was a head-on collision,' she said to Bill. 'She hasn't moved since I got here.' Apparently Carol had been thrown through a windshield. A doctor explained that there was injury to the brain shelf.

" 'If she lives,' said Mrs. Vinall, 'they say she might not be . . . normal.'

"Bill knew that he ought to pray. He was their minister. But what should he pray?

"He looked at Carol and felt that the doctor's guess of an hour was overlong. The girl still had her clothes on; her black sweater was torn and stained. Her hair, pulled back from her torn and bruised face, was matted with blood. The emergency stitches holding the cuts together were swollen and angry.

"And the worst of the injuries, he knew, he could not see at all. Deep inside her skull the bone shelf which supported her brain was fractured. What damage was there to the brain itself? Did he have a right to pray for a physical recovery when there was every chance Carol would become a creature more like a vegetable than like a human? Yet, surely he could not pray that she die.

"Bill approached the girl and placed his hands on the one portion of her body which seemed unhurt, her right arm. Human, negative thoughts crowded in on him, 'Lord,' he said, 'help me to know how to pray.'

"And right away a verse of Scripture popped into Bill's mind. *'We do not* even know how we ought to pray, but through our inarticulate groans the Spirit himself is pleading for us, and God who searches our inmost being knows what the Spirit means. . ." (Romans 8:26, 27 NEB).

"How perfectly the verses fit! Bill took a deep breath and began to pray not with his mind but with his lips and tongue only, bypassing all the doubts and hesitations of his humanity, using the sounds which God gave him. He turned the prayer over entirely to the Holy Spirit, knowing that He loved Carol more than any human could. Bill sensed a strange paradox in the situation: to the degree that he could become passive and yielding, that was the degree to which he could become an effective channel for God.

"Bill prayed with the Spirit this way, quietly and under his breath, for fifteen or twenty minutes. He was only vaguely aware of the room around him; of the standing lamp which threw its beam against the wall, of the bottles of saline solution, the oxygen tent, the jars of plasma standing near Carol's bed, of the other patient in the room who was looking on in wide-eyed silence. He was conscious of Mrs. Vinall's unstirring vigil. But he was aware above all of two things that were happening inside himself. He felt a current of warmth flow through him to the little girl whose arm he held lightly in prayer. And he was aware of the strange, brilliant certainty growing stronger each moment: the sure knowledge that Carol was going to be well again.

"And then Carol moved.

"That was all. Just one fleeting moment. A whisper of life that touched her small body and then was gone. But it gave Bill Nelson the courage to say the thing which was singing in his heart. The thing that he was sure of. The thing that he knew!

" 'Mrs. Vinall, Carol is going to be all right.'

"Once he had spoken the words they sounded preposterous. How dare he! A nurse bent over the bed, imperturbably carrying out the schedule of respiration and plasma feeding.

"The clock on the wall in the corridor said 3:45. Bill had been there just half an hour: it seemed like so much longer. Mrs. Vinall walked with him to the elevator, as though she wanted to stay close to the only voice of hope she had heard. At the elevator he told her again what he did not understand; Carol was going to get well.

"And Bill was right.

"Twelve weeks later, Carol was back in school. Today, five years after the accident, the only after-effects are some hair-fine scars on Carol's face and arms. It is as true today, Bill Nelson believes, as it was when Paul wrote to the Romans, that when we do not know how to pray, 'the Spirit comes to the aid of our weakness.' "[13]

To this I add my personal testimony. I had struggled for a year after my Bible college graduation to find a field of ministry. Although I did a considerable amount of preaching, I was at loose ends to know exactly what field of ministry God would have me enter.

I was a licensed minister with my denomination, but no particular door seemed to open to me. At the same time an idependent preacher invited me to join forces with him. It would have been easy to accept his offer, but there was an uncertainty about it in my spirit. My own parents were certain this was God's open door for me. But in such matters each man must find the will of God for himself.

One day the crisis hour came. It was at the annual conference of our fellowship. My superior officer, knowing of my unsettled state, had asked me to meet with him and the district board over the matter.

The evening prior to that important meeting I decided to discuss my concern with a brother minister who fully understood all the ramifications of my problem. We were from the same church. Our parents were both closely associated with the independent preacher who had invited me to join him. I felt if anyone could advise me, he could.

Together we sat in his auto overlooking a lake at our campground. For a long time we discussed the problem, considering all the angles, but the longer we talked the farther we seemed to be from the answer.

Then a wonderful thing happened. Suddenly, and without any decision on our part to do it, we found ourselves almost mysteriously agreed in agonizing supplication in the Spirit. Together we travailed in an unknown tongue. How long this lasted I do not know; at least an hour I would guess, possibly two hours. Neither of us knew the mind of the Spirit as He interceded through us, though we had a confidence we were praying in God's will. Then, as suddenly as it came, so suddenly the burden of prayer was gone.

In an instant I knew my future with regard to ministry

was settled. Strangely I did not know the path I was to take, but I knew with absolute certainty that I no longer needed concern myself with it.

At the same time both of us were overwhelmed with a sense of the divine presence which was so real we felt we could almost literally touch the Lord. To say the least, it was one-thirty in the morning when our session finally ended.

Neither space nor time will permit a detailed account of what followed. Suffice it to say, it was as though God walked before me for days, leaving His footprints in the sand for me to follow. A chain of events transpired, some of which were beyond human doing, which launched me into a ministry which has continued for more than forty years.

Truly the Spirit helps our "feeblemindedness."

eight

Tongues for a Sign

The gift of tongues has different functions, depending upon the particular circumstances surrounding its use. When it is manifested upon receiving the Holy Spirit it serves as an introduction to the supernatural on the part of the recipient and becomes evidence to him and possibly to others that he has indeed received the baptism in the Spirit.

When employed in the framework of private devotions, its function is personal edification, which springs from the resulting accelerated worship, prayer and praise.

In the coming together of believers its essential function is edification of the body, but if in any circumstance the unbeliever is exposed to it, whether in the church or out of the church, it may become to him a tremendous sign.

It is with this latter function that we shall now concern ourselves.

Much confusion and many questions have evolved from Paul's instructions to the Corinthians, particularly with reference to 1 Cor. 14:20-25. For example, why does he say in verse 22, "tongues are for a sign . . . to them that believe not," and then in verse 23, "If . . . all speak with tongues, and there come in those that are unlearned, or unbelievers, will they not say that ye are mad?" And again, why does he say in verse 22, "prophesying serveth not for them that believe not, but for them which believe," and in verse 24, "But if all prophesy, and there come in one that believeth not, or one unlearned, he is convinced of all, he is judged of all"?

On the surface it appears he is blatantly contradicting himself. Yet, we rest assured this is in no sense the case. The problem is not one of self-contradiction on Paul's part, but one of understanding on our part. Therefore we must search out the answers.

Attention should first be given to the statement, "Wherefore tongues are for a sign."

The word "wherefore" carries us back to the previous verse wherein Paul makes reference to an Old Testament illustration which is evidently intended to support his thesis that tongues are for a sign. In focus is a passage in Isa. 28:11. A prophecy is directed at Ephraim, indicating God's sign to him in the form of an invasion by the Assyrians who would appear speaking in a manner strange to Ephraim. *The Pulpit Commentary* says: "The Assyrian language, though a Semitic idiom nearly allied to Hebrew, was sufficiently different to sound in the ears of a Jew like his own tongue mispronounced and barbarized."[14]

Paul's point seems to be that as the strange tongue of the invaders would be a sign of God's involvement in what was transpiring in that day, even so the tongues speaking which was now occurring was intended as a sign to any who might be unbelieving, indicating that what was happening was indeed of God.

As is so often the case with Old Testament prophecy, the prediction had an almost immediate fulfillment, but it also had couched within it a futuristic fulfillment, which was only understood as a later Spirit-inspired writer made the connection.

It was not *what* the Assyrians said that made Ephraim

know God was indeed speaking. Rather it was the strange speaking which became God's sign in that day.

Likewise, there is no evidence in Scripture to support the idea that God's sign to the unbeliever was His hearing the gospel through a supernatural tongue. But the tongues speaking itself was to be the sign.

Tongues speaking we understand to mean speaking in a language unknown to the speaker. It may or may not be understood by the hearer. When it is understood by the hearer who is an unbeliever, it becomes a powerful sign to him.

Both early church history and contemporary experience bear witness to this.

On the day of Pentecost, upon having received the Holy Spirit, the 120 began to speak with other tongues as the Spirit gave them utterance. A great crowd of onlookers soon arrived and beheld this unusual phenomenon. Deeply puzzled, they cried out, "And how hear we every man in our own tongue, wherein we were born?" (Acts 2:11).

The sign captured the ear of the unbeliever. How could he gainsay it? How could he explain it? There was no way he could lightly write it off. It did in fact strike a death blow at his unbelief and cause him to willingly give ear to the gospel which Peter then so effectively proclaimed.

Affidavits abound on the contemporary scene showing the meaningful function of tongues for a sign. I can share only a few here.

W.F.P. Burton, long a missionary to the Congo, gave some inspiring accounts which illustrate my point well.

"We used to hold gospel services beside Lytham lifeboat house on Sunday evenings.

"One Sunday when a big crowd was listening to the

preaching, the power of God fell on a Mrs. Whiteside, and she began to speak in a strange language. This dear sister would certainly not mind my stating that under ordinary circumstances she was far from grammatical, even in her own language, and had never learned any other.

"As she spoke I found that I could understand all she was saying. A solemn silence fell on the crowd as Mrs. Whiteside spoke in tongues, and I gave the interpretation in English.

"Directly we had finished, a big, middle-aged man stepped into the ring of listeners, and falling on his knees, cried mightily to God to save his soul. He had been a prominent tailor in Lytham, with a big business, but had lost practically everything through his craving for spirits. He was more often inebriated than sober, but now he was as sober as a judge and declared that every word of that utterance in tongues and interpretation went straight to his heart.

"Now it happened that a young Japanese man, who was studying ship building in Lytham ship-building yard, had stood listening among the crowd outside the lifeboat house.

"He went home and asked his landlady, 'Who are those people who preach and sing on Lytham beach?'

"She replied, 'They are a lot of fanatical, religious enthusiasts. Some say they are religion-mad.'

" 'Well, they may be mad,' he remarked, 'but I heard a most remarkable thing. One spoke in perfect Japanese, while another gave the exact equivalent in English.'

"There one had both the tongue and the interpretation corroborated, while the result, in a soul won for the Lord Jesus, was ample evidence that the thing was from God.

"Twice I have heard Kiluba spoken by Spirit-filled be-lievers in England. This is a Central African language, and Sister Durham and Donald Gee, who spoke it, had had no opportunity of learning it. It was in joy and praise to the Lord Jesus."

In a letter dated January 10, 1976, Maxine E. Brewer of Canton, Ohio, wrote to me of a recent remarkable experience which occurred in Jerusalem.

"While we were in Jerusalem, Israel, on one of our trips to the old city, we went to the Wailing Wall. As I approached the wall I felt the awesome presence of our God; I felt as if I was walking about two feet above the ground. Many men and women were at the wall, praying and kissing the wall. There were tourists as well as local people, studying the rules of the Torah, stuffing hand-written prayers into the already filled crevices of the ancient rocks. As I laid my hands upon the wall and began to worship God in a very quiet manner, I began to speak in other tongues as the Spirit prayed through me. I sensed the anointing of the Lord upon me. Standing beside me were several Israeli women, praying and kissing the wall. I was aware of them but paid very little attention. I merely glanced their way and did notice one of them looking at me. Apparently she understood the words that I was praying. I was later told that she never took her eyes from my face. After a considerable time of praying and praising the Lord, we left the Wailing Wall and walked some distance, about 500 yards, into the old city, entering at a little dark and narrow street named Chain Street.

"As I was walking along the street with the rest of the group, between thirty-five and forty, looking at the wonders of this very ancient city, suddenly there came running alongside of me an Israeli woman, the one who stood beside me at the Wailing Wall. She grabbed me by the arm and said, 'Shalom.'

"I replied, 'Shalom.'

"With that she started carrying on a conversation with me. She spoke to me; I answered her in a language that I had not learned. She asked me questions, I gave her answers; this continued for some time. The Spirit of God anointed me in such a beautiful and natural way that we talked for some time together as if we were old friends discussing some vital subject. After the conversation we went on for some time, just how long, I cannot say; the Israeli woman raised her hands over her head and said, 'Hallelujah!' A universal word that means Praise the Lord in every language. As I turned to move away she said, 'Shalom.'

"I replied, 'Shalom.' Shalom in Hebrew means hello, goodbye and peace.

"The people that were traveling with us stopped when they heard and saw what was going on. There were a number of ministers with us—Lutheran, Baptist, Salvation Army and Assemblies of God. The Lutheran minister turned to me and asked, 'What was the language that you were speaking to the Israeli woman?'

"I answered him, 'I don't know for sure, but I believe it was Hebrew.'

"He said, 'What do you mean, you don't know for sure, you were conversing with her, and she with you; she understood what you were saying. I was watching her face. You spoke with such confidence you must have known what you were talking about.'

"He looked intently at me for several minutes and then asked, 'Could that be what they call speaking in other tongues?'

"'Yes. Yes!' I said, 'this is that which was spoken by the prophet Joel; this was the Holy Spirit speaking through me in a language that I have not learned.'

"He said, 'I have never in my life witnessed anything

to compare to this that we have just seen and heard.' And neither had I."

But what of 1 Cor. 14:23 which seems to negate what Paul has said in the previous verse? In verse 22 he plainly says, "Tongues are for a sign . . . to them that believe not." Now he seems to be saying tongues speaking in the congregation will cause the unbeliever present to "say that ye are mad."

It appears to me we must recapture what Paul envisions in order to arrive at an acceptable understanding of his meaning.

Is he not thinking in verse 23 of a gathering of the Corinthian assembly wherein the whole service is given over to the single exercise of tongues speaking, with perhaps no room even given for interpretation? Everyone present, with the exception of the unlearned or unbelievers in such a case, would be carried away with supernatural utterance whereby in the spirit they were speaking mysteries (see 1 Cor. 14:2).

It is doubtful if in any way the sign function of tongues could have applied in that situation. The fact was that quite likely, in Paul's thinking, all present would be Corinthians. There would be no possiblity for the charismatic Corinthians to speak supernaturally in a language unknown to themselves but known to other Corinthian visitors.

Therefore, the noncharismatics present would consider what they were witnessing complete confusion and write off the whole thing as the ranting of a lot of fanatics.

Paul's purpose was to give the Corinthians a sound base for the manifestation of the tongues gift in the church. Yes, there was a meaningful function of tongues as a sign gift, given the proper setting. But in the Corinthian assembly, if the gift was to be meaningful to the Corinthian believers, it would have to be governed by the directives he was giving. Mass use of the gift would not serve that purpose.

What then of prophecy? Wholesale tongues speaking when the whole church is come together is ruled out, but not prophesying.

The general function of the gift of prophecy is geared to the edifying of the church, as is the case with tongues, provided they are interpreted. "But he that prophesieth speaketh unto men to edification and exhortation, and comfort. He that speaketh in an unknown tongue edifieth himself, but he that prophesieth edifieth the church. I would that ye all spake with tongues, but rather that ye prophesied: for greater is he that prophesieth than he that speaketh with tongues, except he interpret, that the church may receive edifying" (1 Cor. 14:3-5).

I repeat, the general function of the gift of prophecy is the edification of the church. Thus Paul says, "prophesying serveth . . . for them which believe."

Nevertheless, unlike wholesale tongues speaking, which can only frighten and turn off the unbeliever, prophecy, though it is essentially for the church, may have a very profound effect upon the visiting unlearned man or unbeliever.

In the case of tongues speaking such an individual would not profit because his understanding would be totally unfruitful. But in the case of prophesying the results might be vastly different since the visitor would be able to understand what was being said. And further, prophecy might well take the form of an exhortation by which he could be brought to an awareness of his own spiritual need. ". . . he is convinced of all, he is judged of all: and thus are the secrets of his heart made manifest; and so falling down on his face he will worship God, and report that God is in you of a truth" (1 Cor. 14:24-25).

Our conclusion then is this. There is a definite place for tongues as a sign to the unbeliever. Tongues speaking in itself may be no sign whatever to him if he does not understand what he is hearing. But when he hears an individual, who not knowing his language, speak in his own language the wonderful works of God, the sign is bound to make a solid impact.

Therefore, tongues speaking is not to be practiced in the coming together of the church apart from the spelled-out guidelines, which require a limit on the number of utterances, as well as interpretation of each utterance (see 1 Cor. 14:27-28).

Prophesying, on the other hand, may be practiced broadly in the church, for it not only serves to edify the body, but it may also prove to be the means of converting the sinner.

nine

Utterance Gifts for Guidance

Not a few theologians and Bible scholars have held differing views on Paul's decision to go to Jerusalem in the face of repeated witness by the Spirit "that bonds and afflictions abide me" (Acts 20:23). Some insist—and they feel they have ample supportive evidence—that Paul arbitrarily rejected the Spirit's directive and thus became the unnecessary victim of deep-seated Jewish antagonism. Others as positively insist—and not without what they deem to be sound biblical support—that Paul went to Jerusalem with full divine approbation.

Much of the argument hangs on views relating to the historical record in Acts 21:4, "And finding disciples, we tarried there seven days; who said through the Spirit, that he should not go up to Jerusalem." The not-too-easily-answered question is, "Did Paul, in this instance, receive an absolute and unmistakable directive, or should this passage be understood some other way?"

Related to the question is the whole matter of guidance through utterance gifts. Consideration of so vital a topic seems especially apropos in an hour when the practice of guidance by gifts is widespread in the land.

At the outset, it is of consequence that historically the utterance gifts have had a commonality with significant outpourings of the Holy Spirit. We need look no further than to the first documentary of the early Church, the Acts of the Apostles, to support this premise. At the initial instance of the Holy Spirit's outpourings in the upper room, the utterance gifts made their immediate appearance. "And they were all filled with the Holy Ghost, and began to speak with other tongues, as the Spirit gave them utterance" (Acts 2:4). The gift of prophecy seems also to be evident on the same occasion in Peter's sermon.

Elsewhere in the Acts is additional evidence. When the Spirit fell upon the Gentiles at the military base in Caesarea, "they heard them speak with tongues and magnify God" (Acts 10:46). Also at Ephesus, under the ministry of Paul, "the Holy Ghost came on them; and they spake with tongues and prophesied" (Acts 19:6).

Action usually spawns reaction. Similarly spiritual declension often sets the stage for spiritual renewal. Ups and downs are as common to the aliveness and vitality of the Church as is temperature change to the passing seasons. The Church was less than a century old when her fervor waned and the once "high voltage" manifestations of the Spirit, as someone has called them, gave way to lesser forms.

Then came the Montanists. It was only the second century after Christ when this revival movement broke upon the scene. With it came a fresh outpouring of the Holy Spirit and subsequently the gifts of prophecy and healing.

According to H.M. Evans, Tertullian, the "Pentecostal of Carthage," a prominent leader of the group, "believed in prophecy, the charismata, and prophetic enthusiasm, and had a personal interest in the matter."[16]

History hints at continuing ups and downs in the passing cycles of Church experience, but in the nineteenth century, the British Isles felt the impact of a spiritual awakening which bore marks of similarity to the first Pentecost. And again the utterance gifts appeared.

Moving forward, the Pentecostal movement was born near the turn of the twentieth century, and with it came a revival of interest in the Holy Spirit, with particular emphasis on the idea that speaking with tongues is the initial physical evidence that one has indeed been baptized in the Spirit. Not only has the movement been concerned with revival of the utterance gifts, but an unmistakable fervor for world evangelization gripped the adherents. The impact has been felt around the world.

But the end was not yet. While the old-line denominations were generally to discount the genuineness of the Pentecostal movement and to write off adherents who espoused their teachings and practices, a new thing was to come upon them with the birth of the charismatic movement. Within a decade every major denomination felt its force. And instead of rejection, charismatics have at least been countenanced, if not warmly welcomed, by those whose previous stance would not have permitted it.

The particular identifying marks of the new movement are quite in harmony with those of other Holy Spirit revivals. Much attention is given to the work of the Spirit in the believer's life. And gifts of the Spirit are not merely recognized; they flourish.

A careful examination of the historical evidence relating to these outpourings of the Holy Spirit reveals a certain chronology of happenings: (1) The Holy Spirit is poured out upon individuals and groups; (2) Immediately thereafter the gifts of the Spirit (particularly the utterance gifts) appear; and (3) Misuse of the utterance gifts sets in, which is the seed of the movement's ultimate ineffectiveness and death unless the misuse is corrected by sound biblical teaching.

Look at the record. The Church was scarcely three decades old when Paul confronted the third stage at

Corinth. Without doubt the Holy Spirit had fallen in that Grecian community. And with the visitation came the gifts of the Spirit. ". . . ye come behind in no gift" (1 Cor. 1:7). Nevertheless, as surely as the gifts appeared, so surely abuse and misuse followed. It was the good fortune of the Corinthians, and of all charismatics of all ensuing periods for that matter, that the mighty teacher Paul was on the scene to recover the church from the folly of its own ignorance.

Would to God that all succeeding Pentecostal groups had had a Paul to guide them past the dangerous pitfalls. And perhaps they did, but in their white-hot fervor they failed to heed the Pauline guidelines; or at least they may not have understood.

The Montanists and Irvingites were not unlike the Corinthians. The Holy Spirit fell upon them, the utterance gifts appeared, and sadly but surely enough, misuses followed. Being so far removed from the Montanists, it is not easy to discover why the movement eventually died. A clue may be found in the previously mentioned article by H.M. Evans. He says, "He [Tertullian] and those who joined him were associated with the churches of the New Prophecy and apparently read the oracles of these prophets along with other Christian writings circulated at this time."[17] Could it be they resorted to the utterance gifts for guidance?

Not so difficult to evaluate is the Irvingite movement. The chronology of experience seems identical to those before. At a point in time the gift of prophecy became the central focus of the movement, much the same as tongues speaking had enamored the Corinthians, only guidance and correction were lacking. Eventually the purported prophetic utterance became the authority for all action, even above Holy Writ, and this proved to be the Irvingites' undoing.

Twentieth-century Pentecostalism has not escaped its predecessors' chronology of experience, except that it, like the Corinthians, has to this point weathered the storms. Indeed there have been misuse and abuse of the utterance gifts, and the Pentecostals themselves do not hesitate to admit it. But the movement's salvation has lain in its avowed acceptance of the sacred Scriptures above every other voice or gift, as the infallible guide for faith and practice, coupled with the ministry of able and gifted teachers who were on hand to guide it through the treacherous waters.

Of concern now is the charismatic movement, with all its freshness and vigor. Lurking in the shadows for many of these delightful people is the temptation to go it alone, not giving due attention to the voice of experience, nor even to guidelines of Scripture. Upon these we urge the greatest caution, lest unpleasant history repeat itself.

Laying a proper foundation of understanding regarding the functions of the utterance gifts can be a very meaningful step toward a sound concept relating to the problem of gifts for guidance. With this the Apostle Paul has provided invaluable assistance. For he, in seeking to aid the Corinthians in reaching a sound position and practice of the utterance gifts, defined their functions.

Tongues, he says, has one principle purpose—edification—edification of the individual when spoken privately, and edification of the church when spoken publicly along with the companion gift, interpretation. "He that speaketh in an unknown tongue edifieth himself. . . . for greater is he that prophesieth than he that speaketh with tongues, except he interpret, that the church may receive edifying" (1 Cor. 14:4-5).

The word "edify," taken at face value and in harmony

with usages elsewhere in the New Testament, is quite readily understood. It means to be a house builder, i.e. to construct or to confirm. Applied to the individual or church, in the frame of reference under consideration, it means that through the utterance gifts of tongues, interpretation and prophecy, either the individual manifesting the gift (as in the case of tongues) or the group within which the gifts (tongues and interpretation, or prophecy) are manifested is built up spiritually and confirmed in spiritual experience.

The functions of prophecy are clearly set forth—edification, exhortation and comfort. "But he that prophesieth speaketh unto men to edification, exhortation and comfort" (1 Cor. 14:3).

"Exhortation" means imploration, hortation, solace. The word springs from another word, meaning to call near, i.e. to invite or to invoke. Thus, employed as it is by Paul in relation to prophecy, we conclude the idea to be conveyed is that one prophesying is speaking to his hearers with a view to calling them nearer to God, or inviting and urging them forward in their spiritual pursuit.

To "comfort" means to console. It too is related closely to another word, meaning to encourage. This gives an additional slant to prophecy's function. The gift is to bring spiritual uplifting and encouragement in the face of distress or difficult circumstance. In his first Thessalonian epistle, Paul uses the same word when he says, "As ye know how we exhorted and comforted and charged every one of you, as a father doth his children" (1 Thess. 2:11).

Having considered the Pauline insight relating to the function of the utterance gifts, we have discovered no hint that they are intended for guidance. Furthermore, vast experience alerts us to the inherent dangers of such practices.

In my earliest association with Pentecostals, I found it a common practice for a few people to gather in prayer over some need or problem, and along with this to expect a "message in tongues" which, when interpreted, would set forth a solution.

It happened that as a teen-ager I was vexed with eczema for which I could find no cure. After a Sunday morning service a small group of us gathered in a side room of the church to obtain guidance from God for handling my problem. Following a "message in tongues," the "interpretation" instructed me to take the juice of carrots and apply it to my eczema-ridden flesh. And I did it in all good faith, but to no avail.

I recall, too, an incident shared by one of my college instructors. He told of a prayer group which met in private houses on a weekly basis. The group was in need of a piano. On a certain evening, while they met in the home of one of the ladies, a young man gave a "message in tongues." His father followed with an "interpretation" in which the lady of the house was instructed to give her piano to the group. When the meeting ended, the lady indicated her perplexity. She said, "I just don't understand. That piano doesn't belong to me. It is borrowed!"

Cases of this kind are not altogether rare. Surely they make some people question and doubt.

But shall we play ostrich in the face of such abuses and misuses? Would it not be better simply to recognize the subtleties of the human frame, which is subject to vanity and error, and go on to discern what the Scripture teaches on the subject?

There is little, if any, direct instruction on the use of supernatural gifts for guidance. At best, we find a few biblical examples of what appears to be a form of guidance. The absence of such instruction could be interpreted as an indication of intent on God's part—that is, that the gifts of tongues, interpretation and prophecy, at least generally, are not intended for guidance. As we have already seen, each of these gifts has its own biblical function.

When it is understood that the essential function of the gift of tongues is edification through prayer, praise, worship and thanksgiving, and that the essential function of prophecy is edification, exhortation and comfort, the danger of misuse is substantially diminished.

I will not say categorically that God cannot give guidance through supernatural utterance gifts, for that would be to deny the possibility of a miracle. But I will say there is no conclusive evidence in Scripture that the utterance gifts are intended for guidance.

The "message in tongues" concept does lend itself readily to the idea of a special message from God to man. And when this concept is espoused, the idea of receiving divine guidance by this means is easily entertained.

Those who accept this concept and endorse its practice may support their view, to their own satisfaction, with certain Scriptures.

But there is much evidence in Acts to support a totally different idea—that is, that the Holy Ghost often spoke directly to individuals, either by a strong inward impression or inner voice.

Note a few examples. "Then the Spirit said unto Philip, Go near and join thyself to this chariot" (Acts 8:29). "And while Peter thought on the vision, the Spirit said unto him, Behold three men seek thee. Arise therefore, and get thee down, and go with them, doubting nothing; for I have sent them" (Acts 10:19-20); "After they were come to Mysia, they assayed to go into Bithynia; but the Spirit suffered them not" (Acts 16:7).

Guidance by similar means is quite common to Spirit-filled Christians today. In a church I pastored was a talented young man who was a victim of leukemia. A group of the church people, including the boy's parents, met for an extended time of fasting and prayer in his behalf. After hours of earnest entreaty, a remarkable sense of God's presence was witnessed. And along with it came a strange sense that praying should now end. All who were present seemed to hear the Spirit speak, though there was no audible voice. In my own spirit a message rang loud and clear, "David is going to die." I hardly dared say anything for I did not wish to add sorrow upon sorrow for the anxious parents. (I have since wondered if the parents themselves had the same witness, but could hardly accept it.) Soon everyone left the place of prayer except an elderly gentleman and myself. He came to me, not knowing what I had heard the Spirit say, and in very gentle tones said, "Brother Brandt, David is going to die."

Thereafter I could no longer pray from my heart for the boy's recovery. I had heard from the Spirit of God and what I heard was confirmed by my elder brother (and later by the boy's decease), yet no utterance gift was in operation.

Nonetheless, it is agreed, there are some problem passages which must be examined. A classic example is Acts 13:2. "As they ministered to the Lord and fasted, the Holy Ghost said, Separate me Barnabas and Saul for the work whereunto I have called them." The question arises, "How did the Holy Ghost speak?" Was it through tongues and interpretation? Was it by prophecy? Or was it by yet another means?

If we accept the concept that tongues speaking is always unto God, the idea that the Holy Ghost spoke to the Church by this means is ruled out.

Further, if we adhere to the Pauline idea that prophecy is for edification, exhortation and comfort, again we find little room for assigning the Holy Ghost directive to the gift of prophecy. However, it is conceivable that the command to "separate me Barnabas and Saul" could be classed as an exhortation. We do not rule out this possibility.

Therefore, the possibility exists that in the case of Barnabas and Saul, indicated in Acts 13:2, the Holy Ghost did not employ an utterance gift, but rather spoke to an individual, perhaps an elder, and through him to the assembled group.

At best, the only evidence at hand indicates only by inference the use of one or more spiritual gifts in this instance. But there is no conclusive evidence.

Furthermore, regardless of how the Spirit's command was forthcoming, it should not be overlooked that what was said was not strictly guidance. It was rather confirmation of guidance already received, "Separate me Barnabas and Saul unto the work whereunto I have called them." The calling had evidently come to them individually and personally. Now the confirmation came publicly.

I would be extremely cautious of any directive given to an individual for his personal life or ministry through utterance gifts, and would place no credence upon such a thing unless it was in confirmation of an already recognized inner conviction.

Consideration must also be given to a series of experiences in Paul's life. At a certain juncture he testified, "And now, behold, I go bound in the spirit unto Jerusalem, not knowing the things that shall befall me there: Save that the Holy Ghost witnesseth in every city, saying that bonds and afflictions abide me" (Acts 20:22-23). Shortly thereafter he wrote, "And finding certain disciples, we tarried there seven days: who said to Paul through the Spirit, that he should not go up to Jerusalem" (Acts 21:4). A little later the prophet Agabus enters the picture. "And when he was come unto us, he took Paul's girdle, and bound his own hands and feet, and said, Thus saith the Holy Ghost, So shall the Jews at Jerusalem bind the man that owneth this girdle, and shall deliver him into the hands of the Gentiles" (Acts 21:11).

Again we are confronted with the problem of guidance through the gifts. Three particular statements deserve thoughtful consideration: "the Holy Ghost witnesseth," "who said to Paul through the Spirit" and "Thus saith the Holy Ghost, So shall the Jews at Jerusalem bind the man. . . ." Several questions immediately surface. (1) By what means or in what manner did the Holy Ghost witness? (2) In what way did the Christians at Tyre speak to Paul through the Spirit? (3) What gift did Agabus employ as he addressed Paul?

Some scholars have concluded that in the face of these experiences, Paul made one of the worst mistakes of his Christian life when he went up to Jerusalem. They are confident he most certainly missed the will of God, and that he flagrantly rejected divine guidance. After all, had he not been told plainly not to go up to Jerusalem?

Let us examine each of these passages carefully.

In the first instance (Acts 20:22-23), there is no hint of guidance. There is an element of prediction—"bonds and afflictions abide me." And this same ominous sense of trouble seems to have been in every city Paul visited at this time. How it was communicated is nowhere stated. The only word we have for it is "the Holy Ghost witnesseth." The idea set forth is that the Holy Ghost testified to what was ahead. Was it through tongues and interpretation? Was it by prophecy? Or was it by another means? It is doubtful that any view can be proven conclusively. However, those who have had a fair share of experience with the Holy Spirit readily understand the Spirit's ability to communicate knowledge to the believer apart from any outward manifestation. It is the communication of Spirit with spirit, and it is an almost awesome thing to discover that a common bit of knowledge has been inwardly communicated to not only a single individual but to a group or even to several groups, apart from any oral communication whatsoever.

The second passage (Acts 21:4) is, on the surface, a pure case of divine guidance through a supernatural gift or gifts. Nevertheless, I am quite well persuaded we have here, rather than a clear case of divine guidance through the Spirit, a good example of human interpretation placed upon the inward communication of the Spirit. Surely the Holy Spirit had witnessed to the Christians in Tyre, just as he had in other cities. In their spirits they too perceived that trouble lay ahead for Paul if he went to Jerusalem.

Now this is the precise point of danger. We are prone to mingle inward revelation of the Spirit with our own interpretation based upon mere human sentiment.

The fact is, these Christians dearly loved Paul. They could not bear the idea of his suffering as indicated by the Spirit. Thus they interpreted that which was truly predictive as being intended as a revelation of divine guidance.

There is no doubt that the Tyre Christians had a true inward witness, a revelation of certainties ahead for Paul. Yet there is grave doubt that their application of the revelation was valid. How they spoke to Paul "through the Spirit" is not stated. Possibly it was by prophecy. If so, would not Paul have been under sacred responsibility to comply? The answer is: not necessarily, for there is always the possibility of human error.

There is sound evidence Paul knew what the will of God was already. He knew he was headed for Rome for Luke wrote, "After these things were ended, Paul purposed in his spirit, when he had passed through Macedonia and Achaia, to go to Jerusalem, saying, After I have been there, I must also see Rome" (Acts 19:20).

Thus there must have been in his mind a conflict over this new directive that he should not go up to Jerusalem. The Spirit evidently had said to him, "Go." Now the people are saying to him by the Spirit, "Don't go!" Does he have a right to judge what he has now heard? Indeed he does. In fact we are all under orders to judge, and I believe for the very reason that in these matters human error is always possible. Listen to the Word: "Let the prophets speak two or three, and let the other judge" (1 Cor. 14:29). Add to that, "For we know in part, and we prophesy in part" (1 Cor. 13:9).

You see, it is human nature to save ourselves. No doubt Paul's flesh was tempted by the prophetic directive he got in Tyre. But he was not about to live after the flesh, for he knew a higher law. Had not his Lord said, "For whosoever will save his life shall lose it; but whosoever shall lose his life for my sake and the gospel's, the same shall save it" (Mark 8:35).

In this light I feel safe in concluding that by whatever gift the Tyre Christians spoke to Paul, they were, perhaps unwittingly, substituting direction for information. And there is a vast difference.

We should turn to our Lord's experience at this point, for there is in it a strange parallel to that of Paul at Tyre. "From that time forth began Jesus to shew unto his disciples, how that he must go unto Jerusalem, and suffer many things of the elders and chief priests and scribes, and be killed, and be raised again the third day. Then Peter took him and began to rebuke him, saying, Be it far from thee, Lord: this shall not be unto thee. But he turned, and said unto Peter, Get thee behind me, Satan: thou art an offence unto me: for thou savourest not the things that be of God, but those that be of men" (Matt. 16:21-23).

Jesus had announced to His disciples His coming suffering and death at Jerusalem. This was, we can accurately say, a genuine revelation of the Spirit, since the Spirit of God indwelt Jesus. In essence it was little different than the direct revelation of the Spirit to the Tyre Christians regarding Paul's forthcoming and nearly similar experience.

And, not unlike the Tyre Christians also, the disciples had strong sentiments toward the Lord which produced a purely human reaction to that revelation, which found expression through Peter, and which drew a severe rebuke from the Lord.

There is in all of this a great lesson for us. Let us listen carefully to the Spirit's witness on the one hand, but let us guard against becoming instruments or victims of false direction springing from human sentiment.

What then of Agabus's word in Acts 21:11?

Here is an articulation of what the Spirit was witnessing all along the way. Since Agabus is designated "a certain prophet," we can conclude his recorded words were a prophetic utterance—a manifestation of the gift of prophecy. It should at once be noted that there is no hint of direction, but a clear declaration of what Paul could expect at Jerusalem. Has it occurred to us that had Paul been persuaded to refrain from going to Jerusalem, this prophecy would not have come true?

The reaction in Caesarea (where Paul now was) was the same as in Tyre. "And when we heard these things, both we, and they of that place, besought him not to go up to Jerusalem" (Acts 21:12).

Listen to Paul's response. "What mean ye to weep and to break mine heart? for I am ready not to be bound only but also to die at Jerusalem for the name of the Lord Jesus" (Acts 21:13). Was Paul just a stubborn die-hard who had no regard for God's will? Of course not. The concern of the people deeply distressed him. Yet he was not about to be deterred by mere human sentiment. He would tread the same path His Master had trod over half a century earlier, and nothing would change his mind.

Finally human sentiment gave way to the divine will, and Luke records, "And when he would not be persuaded, we ceased, saying, The will of the Lord be done" (Acts 21:14). I think the human will was reflected in the various attempts to persuade, even under the guise of supernatural utterance. Only after the servant of God withstood all of the pressures were the people brought to acquiesce to the will of God.

We conclude then that there is little scriptural support for the concept that spiritual gifts are in any general way intended for imparting divine guidance. But in the event guidance is given by this means, it is the part of wisdom to judge the communication by the Word. The youthful and inexperienced would do well to consult with mature spiritual leaders over direction received through supernatural gifts, and this particularly as it relates to vital decisions affecting life and ministry.

ten

Shall Tongues Cease?

The answer is a positive yes. Paul left no room for doubt when he wrote "whether there be tongues, they shall cease" (1 Cor. 13:8). But the fair question is "When?"

Paul's statement is a handy device for those seeking to support an already firmed-up position. Yet for those who openheartedly pursue truth it is like a lofty mountain beckoning the hardy climber.

If Paul, writing by divine inspiration, was projecting the idea that supernatural tongues speaking would end within a very short time, say a generation, after his letter, it is obvious that modern tongues speaking is merely a counterfeit of the real, and should therefore be rejected. I believe it is accurate to say not a few espouse this view.

On the other hand, if he was simply alluding to the eventual cessation of tongues speaking, there is certainly room, if not good reason, to believe it is intended as a meaningful practice and privilege for the entire Church Age.

A sound scriptural answer must be found.

There is another related question. Was the historical decline of tongues speaking in the early centuries after Christ, plus its nearly total absence for sixteen to seventeen centuries, fulfillment of Paul's prediction, or was this purely the result of diminished spiritual light and life? This too deserves some in-depth research.

Sound hermeneutics would lead us, in the first place, to seek an objective overview of the section of Scripture under consideration.

It is immediately evident that 1 Corinthians 13 was not originally intended to be merely a treatise on love. The chapter forms a vital link between chapters 12 and 14, and is a very meaningful part of the entire discussion relating to spiritual gifts. To lift chapter 13 out of its setting is to miss the central emphasis.

In no way is Paul seeking to discourage, discount, or write off as useless the practice of tongues speaking. His clear purpose, on the contrary, is to make the gift more significant. Love, he says, is the sure foundation to desired meaningfulness. Love, a thing of eternity, will make tongues speaking, a thing of time, worthwhile.

Love encompasses both time and eternity. "Charity [love] never faileth" (1 Cor. 13:8). But the gifts of the Spirit are only bestowals for time. Their limitations, since they operate on the earthly scene and in the human framework, will be replaced by fullness and completeness in eternity. "For we know in part, and we prophesy in part. But when that which is perfect is come, then that which is in part shall be done away" (1 Cor. 13:9-10).

The comparisons in the passage are set forth in the terms "now" and "then." In the "now" there will be prophecy, there will be tongues, there will be the word of knowledge. In the "then" they will be replaced by something better. "For now we see through a glass, darkly; but then, face to face: now I know in part; but then shall I know even as also I am known" (1 Cor. 13:12).

There can be little doubt that Paul is comparing time with eternity. To say that his statement, "whether there be tongues, they shall cease" was intended to mean "cease early in the Church age" is to do violence to his argument. His argument is that these gifts, which are related to time, will cease "when that which is perfect is come." For, "then that which is in part shall be done away." There is no hint that these things shall be done away prior to that time. Instead, they are gifts intended for the spiritual good of all of those related to time.

Some would use verse 11 in support of the idea that Paul was discounting tongues by relegating its use to spiritual infancy or to immaturity. "When I was a child I spake as a child, I thought as a child: but when I became a man, I put away childish things" (1 Cor. 13:11). Nevertheless, such a view conflicts solidly with Paul's own later testimony, "I thank my God, I speak with tongues more than ye all" (1 Cor. 14:18). Thus it is immediately evident he is in no way saying in verse 11 (chapter 13) that tongues is a childish thing.

What then is he saying? He is clearly illustrating his "now" and "then" concept. Childhood, with its many limitations, is a picture of the "now" as it relates to the spiritual gifts. Indeed they are present, even as understanding and thinking are present in a child. Adulthood, on the other hand, with its departure from childish things, and with its maturity in understanding and thinking, is a picture of escape from earthly limitations.

Furthermore, it is the view of some that since tongues speaking is discussed only in the Corinthian epistle, and is not to be found in the many other epistles, its use was confined more or less to that particular group; and therefore it was of little consequence and was to be of short duration.

How easy it is to establish a rationale, particularly to support a bias.

But why not apply the same rationale to the communion service? Where else in the epistles is there a discussion of this blessed ordinance? Dare we say that since it is confined to the single epistle of 1 Corinthians it was really of little consequence and should be considered outdated in its usefulness? Brethren, I think not. The same rationale should be applied to both communion and tongues speaking. Either both are valid and meaningful today, or neither of them is.

It should also be noted that to say tongues speaking is not at all in focus in the other epistles may not be altogether accurate. Certainly tongues speaking is by no means the central thing of importance in the Church. The other epistles concern themselves with the many other facets of the Christian life. The absence of lengthy discussion of glossalalia in them does not necessarily indicate its absence in the other churches. It was handled in the Corinthian epistle because there it was being abused, just as in the Galatian epistle the problem of returning to the bondage of the Law was handled, because that problem existed there.

As I have noted in the chapter "I Will Sing With the Spirit," there is strong evidence to support the idea that Paul had singing in tongues in mind when he wrote, "Speaking to yourselves in psalms and hymns and spiritual songs, singing and making melody in your heart to the Lord" (Eph. 5:19). And indeed it would be strange if tongues speaking was not common in that church, the Ephesian church, since it began with such a charismatic manifestation (see Acts 19:1-6).

Again in the Ephesian epistle Paul wrote, "Praying always with all prayer and supplication in the Spirit" (Eph. 6:18). Supplication in the Spirit most likely applies to praying in tongues.

The same thought seems to have been in Jude's mind when he wrote, "But ye, beloved, building up yourselves on your most holy faith, praying in the Holy Ghost" (Jude 20).

In considering tongues speaking historically, unless careful scrutiny is practiced, it might be concluded that tongues-speaking did indeed cease not too long after the Church began. However, scholars who have researched history have documented cases of tongues speaking from its earliest beginnings in an almost constant manifestation to this present time. That it was scarcely evident at times cannot be denied. Yet the same is true of other doctrines and practices of the church.

For example, the mighty doctrine of justification by faith lay dormant for centuries until Luther relit that glorious candle of truth which lighted the whole world. Surely the fact that justification by faith was lost among the stuff was no valid evidence that the truth had become invalid. Nay, rather it was evidence that the prevailing spiritual climate was as in the days of Samuel—"there was no open vision" (1 Sam. 3:1).

When spiritual hunger had earned the attention of the Almighty, the famishing were fed. It is always so. It was thus when Jesus came. For several hundred years Israel had languished in general spiritual unconcern and poverty. The prophet perceived it when he cried, "For he shall grow up before him as a tender plant, and as a root out of a dry ground" (Isa. 53:2). How dry that "ground" was! Earnest men looked intently for the Messiah, the Consolation of Israel—and He came!

It is no different with the Holy Spirit. If tongues ceased it was because the Holy Spirit was given no place. "Because that when they knew God they glorified him not as God, neither were they thankful; but became vain in their imaginations, and their foolish heart was darkened" (Rom. 1:21).

The Holy Spirit came in the first place to hungry, ready men. When He came, tongues speaking began. And it continued until men neglected the gift they had received. The degree of the cessation was exactly parallel with the degree of true spiritual fervency, until by reason of neglect, the precious jewel of truth was buried from human knowledge and view.

Hungering souls in succeeding ages glimpsed the truth and some tasted of its sweetness, only eventually to be deprived of the glory as a result of the prevailing climate of ignorance and unconcern.

But that condition could not prevail forever. True, groups like the Irvingites of the British Isles came and went, not because they had not seen light, but because of an unfortunate admixture of light and darkness.

Yet, in these last days, God, who knows men's hearts, is pouring out His Spirit upon all flesh as He said He would. Forseeing the day when universally men would again truly hunger for Him and welcome His Spirit in His fullness, He inspired the prophet to write, "I will pour out my spirit upon all flesh; and your sons and your daughters shall prophesy, your old men shall dream dreams, and your young men shall see visions: And also upon the servants and upon the handmaids in those days will I pour out of my spirit" (Joel 2:28-29).

Indeed tongues shall cease, but only after the last hungering child of God has been filled with the Spirit and caught up into the everlasting Kingdom.

eleven

I Will Sing With the Spirit

Singing with the Spirit is as old as the early Church, and as new as the modern charismatic movement. It is a spiritual exercise, which by its very nature may generate a harmony so akin to the divine that it attracts the attention of heaven.

Although I have had some acquaintance with the practice from my earliest association with the Pentecostal movement, I have witnessed much more of it in recent time.

The Apostle Paul left no doubt that singing with the Spirit is an acceptable form of worship. He wrote, *"I will sing with the spirit, and I will sing with the understanding also"* (1 Cor. 14:15).

There is little room to question what he meant by the expression "sing with the spirit." Certainly he meant something beyond mere spirited singing, and also something more than singing out of his emotions. Without question he had in mind singing in an unknown tongue.

Here is his own testimony, "For if I pray in an unknown tongue, my spirit prayeth, but my understanding is unfruitful. What is it then? I will pray with the spirit, and I will pray with the understanding also: I will sing with the spirit, and I will sing with the understanding also" (1 Cor. 14:14-15).

If praying "with the spirit" is praying in an unknown tongue, and this is obvious from the statement, "For if I pray in an unknown tongue, my spirit prayeth," then it is also clear that singing with the spirit is indeed singing in an unknown tongue.

In an article relating to this subject entitled, "What Are 'Spiritual Songs'?" Larry W. Hurtado makes some valuable observations. He notes that F.F. Bruce, when commenting on Eph. 5:18-19, "puts us on what appears to be a . . . fruitful track when he describes spiritual songs as something that 'might be unpremeditated words *sung in the Spirit*, voicing holy aspirations.' "[18]

Hurtado goes on to say, "Bruce's phrase 'in the Spirit' and the reference he cites at this point (1 Corinthians 14:15) both refer in the Corinthian context to singing different from singing 'with the understanding' (*to noi*). It should be clear that in 1 Corinthians 14:15 both praying and singing 'with the understanding' mean basically that the believer is praying and singing out of his own thought life and using his own words to express his prayer or song. Thus praying or singing 'with the Spirit' must correspond to praying or singing at the prompting of the Spirit and using the words supplied by the Spirit. We are in the context then of rapturous worship in which a person finds himself under the sway of the Holy Spirit.

"If it can be granted that 1 Corinthians 14:15 makes room for such singing at the Spirit's prompting and in other tongues, can we make the same claim for Ephesians 5:19? Is singing 'in the Spirit' exactly the same as singing 'in spiritual songs'?

"Other evidence seems to confirm this line of inquiry. Note that the word *spiritual—pneumatikos—*is the same adjective used by Paul in 1 Corinthians 12:1 and 14:1 to describe what is translated 'spiritual gifts.' The word is then used by Paul to refer to the dramatic and supernatural

works of God which include utterances empow
the Spirit. Indeed, in all Paul's use of the word *spi*
must understand the idea of the supernatural
God. Spiritual men are men who are controlle
Holy Spirit. When Paul prays in Ephesians
adoration to the God who has blessed us in Chr
every spiritual blessing' (NASB), he is referrin
specifically Christian blessings of the appropr
Christ's redemption, the adoption into sons
communion with the Godhead, and the mi
power at work in Christians severing them fr
power and rendering them in dramatic ways av
God. All these things are the blessings of the Hc
hence, they are called 'spiritual blessing.'

"It should further be noted that the cc
Ephesians 5:19 contrasts the incoherence of dru
with being filled with the Spirit. The contrast i
not only because Paul puts together two such
states as far as quality is concerned, but als
these two states do have some small similarit
case we are talking about a person giving hims
the influence of another stimulus other that
will—either copious amounts of wine or satu
the Spirit! This means that we are in the co
contrast between carnal and spiritual ecstasy.
the debauchery of wine, Christians are to be
the Spirit, allowing themselves to be controll
even to the extent of rapturous worship ir
songs, and carried away with thankfulness
and complete because it is prompted by th
God."

Harold Horton gives some additional light: '
to yourselves in . . . spiritual songs,' that i
other tongues sung to cadences dictated a

Spirit. Speaking—in song! Speaking to ourselves thus in the Spirit is edifying ourselves, just as, to use the figure of the previous verse, drinking wine to ourselves is inebriating ourselves. Being filled with the Spirit and yielding to the sweet exercise of speaking or singing with other tongues is building up ourselves, as well as magnifying the Lord and making melody to Him in our hearts (1 Cor. 14:15).

"If we speak with tongues we have a well within us in this barren wilderness of a world. Singing thus will start a fountain in the driest desert, 'Spring up, O well; Sing ye unto it!' Yes: sing unto the gushing fountain within: so shall its refreshing waters increase."[19]

What are the advantages of singing in a language unknown to one's self?

At very best the human is limited and weak. And though man be regenerated through the new birth he remains unable to attain the heights he envisions. This he reveals in his songs. We hear him sing:

> Lord, lift me up and let me stand,
> By faith, on heaven's table land,
> A higher plane than I have found;
> Lord, plant my feet on higher ground.

And Charles Wesley expressed it so meaningfully when he wrote,

> O for a thousand tongues to sing
> My great Redeemer's praise,
> The glories of my God and King,
> The triumphs of His grace.

The gift of tongues is God's answer to man's deepest need. Through it he is enabled to transcend human limitations and to reach an entirely new plane of

expression. The reason for this is that he is drawing upon the limitless ability of God's own Spirit.

Illustrations out of life are often helpful aids in our seeking to understand truth. Mrs. Ruth Carter (formerly Mrs. Wesley R. Steelberg) shared this enlightening account: "In 1906 my father (Elmer Fisher), who had been a Baptist pastor, received the baptism in the Holy Spirit. The following year he opened a Pentecostal work which became known as the Upper Room Mission. His motto was, 'Exalt Jesus Christ; honor the Holy Ghost.' There was revival for many years in the mission, with two services a day, five days a week. The morning Bible studies were conducted by George Studd, a gifted, Spirit-filled Bible teacher, brother of the famous missionary C.T. Studd.

"The Upper Room Mission was in a large hall on Mercantile Place (which later became an arcade) between Spring and Broadway, and Fifth and Sixth, in the heart of Los Angeles.

"One Sunday afternoon in the fall of 1913, God moved in an unusual way in the service. I was only a girl, seated beside my mother on the front seat. As the blessing of the Lord began to fall like dew during the song service, the people began to worship in the Spirit. There were several hundred present, and all seemed oblivious to everyone else as they worshipped. The sacred Presence was so real that one after another the people stood to their feet, hands upraised, eyes closed, lost in worship.

"The chorus of praise began to unite them. Even those who ordinarily were hardly able to carry a tune sang like opera singers. Then it blended into such harmony, without a discordant note. It was what we called the 'heavenly choir.' As the cadences of this supernatural song rose and fell, the beauty of it was beyond description.

"I had always loved the Lord, but I had not yet been filled with the Spirit. Now my heart too was full of worship, but I was very timid. If I stood to praise the Lord, someone might see me. However, as far as I could see, all had their eyes closed. I reasoned that I too could stand and praise Him whom my soul loved, then sit down before anyone else did, and no one would notice me. So I stood.

"I cannot explain what happened. I only know that I was utterly unconscious of my surroundings as I joined in that heavenly chorus, lost in adoration as my soul reached out to Him.

"When I opened my eyes everyone was seated, and I sat down hastily. Later I learned I had been standing alone for some time, worshipping in the language of heaven. The people, after the heavenly song had ceased, had been seated, and waited quietly in the presence of One who had filled a little girl with His Holy Spirit. Something else was also accomplished in that meeting where program was set aside while the Spirit moved, though it was several years later that I heard the story.

"A man who had been healed of blindness under my father's ministry held a meeting in the church my husband (the late Wesley R. Steelberg) served as pastor. He told of having been in the service that afternoon in 1913. He was sitting toward the back of the hall when a stranger came in and sat beside him. Later he learned that the man was a music teacher—and an agnostic. He had been walking along the street below the open windows of the hall when he heard singing. He stopped to listen—such harmony, such blending of chords he had never heard. Whatever could it be, he wondered. Finding the stairway, he came up to this large auditorium, seating himself beside our friend. He sat entranced until the music ceased. Then a conversation something like this followed;

" 'What is this?'

" 'This is a gospel meeting.'

" 'But who taught the people to sing like that?'

" 'No one taught them. It is God.'

" 'But how did they learn such harmony?'

" 'They did not learn it; it was given by the Holy Spirit.'

"The stranger could not understand it, but sitting in that hall with God's presence so real, he felt there *must* be a God. The singing he had heard had some supernatural quality. It would take God to do that.

"Under deep conviction he yielded his life to God. It is possible that no preaching could have convinced him of his need as the Holy Spirit did that afternoon through a congregation yielded to Him."[20]

And from Dick Eastman comes this exciting account: "Those involved in the all-night prayer vigil were sitting quietly in worship when one softly began to sing in a strange-sounding language. Soon the majority were singing in various heavenly languages, as suggested by Paul in 1 Corinthians 14:15.

"Little could equal the beauty of such singing. And I would have admitted it sounded God-sent even if I hadn't heard the amazing testimony of a young student from India. According to the youth, the voice beginning the singing that night sang a special chant used only by priests in the Eastern Orthodox Church in which the lad grew up. The chanting melody—with the words—from a special part of their religious service. The chant is a 'praise chant' used only during the part of the service when praise is offered. The Indian youth had listened that night to a miracle. He had become just one more participant in a revival of God's *power* and *glory*."[21]

Singing with the Spirit may take on different forms. I have witnessed a single individual sing in tongues on several occasions. At the conclusion of an evening service in the old Southside Assembly in Springfield, Missouri, a lady, sitting a long way back in the long auditorium, burst forth singing with the Spirit in such beautiful tones that the whole audience was electrified. Upon inquiring I learned she had never done this before. An old-timer testified he had not witnessed anything to compare to this in fifty years in Pentecostal circles.

Sometimes two or more have joined their voices in singing with the Spirit. G. Raymond Carlson, assistant general superintendent of the Assemblies of God, related to me some details of such an incident. During a youth camp many young people had crowded into a prayer room seeking to be baptized in the Spirit. Suddenly and simultaneously two young people, far removed from each other, were baptized in the Spirit, whereupon each of them began singing the identical words in tongues, and to the identically same tune.

Attending modern charismatic and Pentecostal gatherings it is not at all uncommon to hear an entire audience singing with the Spirit. There is no learned melody or common lyric. Yet there is often the variety, the flow, the harmony, and the blend of a mighty choir. And more than that there is an accompanying sense that God is indeed inhabiting the praises of His people.

I think this is significant. There is reason to believe that God is a being of perfect harmony. There is nothing discordant about His nature or His character. I am confident that the original creation was a perfectly harmonious thing, reflecting its great Creator.

Because harmony is His very nature, it is not difficult to understand that Spirit-induced harmony in the midst of His children would invite a special manifestation of His all-glorious Presence. Did not David cry out, "Deep calleth unto deep at the noise of thy waterspouts" (Ps. 42:7)?

This heavenly response to harmony, when it is found among God's children, is beautifully set forth by Jesus. Speaking to His disciples, He declared: "Again I say unto you, That if two of you shall agree on earth as touching any thing that they shall ask, it shall be done for them of my Father which is in heaven" (Matt. 18:19). The Greek word *sumphonia*, which is translated "agree" in this text, springs from a root meaning to symphonize or harmonize. And the idea being set forth is that if only two can find themselves symphonizing or harmonizing in mind and spirit they can be sure God will respond with heaven's resources. Such harmony attracts Him like a magnet attracts a metal similar to itself. Thus it is with singing with the Spirit. Its dividends are rich.

The question logically arises, How can I sing with the Spirit? Must I wait until some overwhelming impulse launches me into this new dimension in spiritual expression, or is there something I can personally do to enjoy this blessing?

I am persuaded most of us come far short of God's best, not only in the area of singing with the Spirit, but in all areas of Christian experience, for two principal reasons. The first of these is inadequate or imperfect knowledge. The second is unbelief. Until we know, we can hardly believe. When we know, we must either believe or fall short of God's provision.

Paul has a word to help us. He says, "I will pray with the spirit, and I will pray with the understanding also: I will sing with the spirit, and I will sing with the understanding also" (1 Cor. 14:15-16). The key word is "*I will.*"

Praying and singing with the Spirit result from an act of the will. God does not impose any of His gifts upon us. When we have received the baptism in the Holy Spirit, we have within us the potential for these blessed spiritual exercises, but even then their manifestation is governed by the degree of our knowledge, and our willingness to launch out in simple faith.

I know how to swim and I have every confidence the water will carry me when I yield myself to it. But it never happens apart from an act of my will. Likewise I do not sing with the Spirit until I will to do it.

In the light of Paul's instruction to the Ephesians there is room to believe that he looked upon singing with the Spirit as a godly exercise for both the individual and for the body of believers corporately. The clear inference is that this would be a consequence of the Spirit-filled life. "And be not drunk with wine, wherein is excess; but be filled with the Spirit; Speaking to yourselves in psalms and hymns and spiritual songs, singing and making melody in your heart to the Lord" (Eph. 5:18-19).

The Promise of the Father

The baptism in the Holy Spirit is identified in several ways in Scripture. A whole list of terms refers to but a single experience:

1) "promise of the Father" (Acts 1:4)
2) "baptized with the Holy Ghost" (Acts 1:5)
3) "after that the Holy Ghost is come upon you" (Acts 1:8)
4) "filled with the Holy Ghost" (Acts 2:4)
5) "the gift of the Holy Ghost" (Acts 2:38)
6) "they received the Holy Ghost" (Acts 8:17)
7) "the Holy Ghost fell on them" (Acts 10:44)
8) "because that on the Gentiles also was poured out the gift of the Holy Ghost" (Acts 10:45)
9) "the Holy Ghost came on them" (Acts 19:6)

Each of these terms—"baptized with," "is come upon you," "filled with," "the gift of," "they received," "fell on them," "was poured," and "came on them"—casts its own ray of light on a common experience. And from this we should understand that no human terminology is adequate to fully express the experience.

In this chapter our particular concern is with the first listed above, "the promise of the Father."

This is a curious term, employed in this form only by Luke, but loaded with significance.

In his gospel Luke says, quoting the Lord, "And behold, I send the promise of my Father upon you: but tarry ye in Jerusalem, until ye be endued with power from on high" (Luke 24:49).

Again in the Acts, Luke writes, "And, being assembled together with them, commanded them that they should not depart from Jerusalem, but wait for the promise of the Father, which, saith he, ye have heard of me" (Acts 1:4).

Through this single phrase, "promise of the Father," a beautiful link is discovered between the baptism in the Holy Ghost and the original promise made to Abram (later known as Abraham) as recorded in Genesis.

At first thought this connection may seem of little significance. Yet, some in-depth consideration will show it to be of prime importance.

The Pauline epistle to the Galatians spans the whole period from Abraham to Christ, and excitingly expounds the connection between these two highly significant persons.

In introducing the intriguing subject, Paul wrote, "Christ hath redeemed us from the curse of the law" (Gal. 2:13) for the express purpose "that the blessing of Abraham might come on the Gentiles through Jesus Christ" (Gal. 3:14). And then, as if to clarify his specific meaning of the term "blessing of Abraham," he adds, "that we might receive the promise of the Spirit through faith."

A bit later Paul relates the promise of the Spirit to a promise of inheritance. "For if the inheritance be of the law, it is no more of promise: but God gave it to Abraham by promise" (Gal. 3:18).

Now, "the promise of the Spirit" should not be interpreted as "a promise made by the Spirit," for that would completely change the sense.

The Holy Spirit is not merely the agent of a promised

118

inheritance. Instead, He is in some very significant way the inheritance itself. ". . . after that ye believed, ye were sealed with that Holy Spirit of promise, which is the earnest of our inheritance until the redemption of the purchased possession, unto the praise of his glory" (Eph. 1:13-14).

"Now," says Paul, "to Abraham and his seed were the promises made" (Gal. 3:16). It will be advantageous to pinpoint the Old Testament Scriptures to which Paul has reference. "And the Lord said unto Abram, after that Lot was separated from him, Lift up now thine eyes, and look from the place where thou art northward, and southward, and eastward, and westward: For all the land which thou seest, to thee will I give it, and to thy seed for ever. And I will make thy seed as the dust of the earth: so that if a man can number the dust of the earth, then shall thy seed also be numbered" (Gen. 13:16). "And he brought him forth and said, Look now toward heaven, and tell the stars, if thou be able to number them: and he said unto him, So shall thy seed be" (Gen. 15:5).

Thus, the promises to Abraham are seen to be essentially twofold. First is the promise of land—Canaan—and second is the promise of vast posterity.

But from Paul's enlightened viewpoint, the promises, although on the surface they have only to do with the earthly and physical, beneath the surface inculcate the heavenly and spiritual. On the surface the seed is natural Israel. Beneath the surface the seed is Christ and spiritual Israel. On the surface the inheritance is Canaan land; beneath the surface, the inheritance is the Spirit-filled life now, and ultimately the eternal state.

Even Abraham seems to have glimpsed the difference, "for he looked for a city, which hath foundations, whose builder and maker is God" (Heb. 11:10).

But back to the promise. Paul makes a special point of the fact that the promise was first given to Abraham, and then beyond Abraham it was extended directly to Christ. "He saith not, And to seeds, as of many; but as of one. And to thy seed, which is Christ" (Gal. 3:16).

The particular emphasis is on "seed" rather than "seeds."

Thus the promise is narrowed down in its spiritual fulfillment to only one person, Christ. Why? Why should the promise of the Spirit be made to Christ? Why should the inheritance converge strictly upon Him?

The very valid reason is that He is the Head of the Church, which does not exist apart from Him, and which receives nothing from the Father save through Him. As the human body receives air, water and nourishment through the head, likewise all that the Body of Christ receives from the Father, it must receive through "the head, from which all the body by joints and bands having nourishment ministered, and knit together, increaseth with the increase of God" (Col. 2:19).

Keeping in mind the words of Jesus to His disciples, "And, behold, I send the promise of my Father upon you" (Luke 24:49), we now discover the actual fulfillment, noting in particular the sequence of events.

Let us remind ourselves once more of the sequence indicated by Paul to the Galatians: First, the promise was made to Abraham. Second, it was made to Abraham's seed, which is summed up in one person, Christ. But, this is not the end, for Paul says it encompasses all who are in Christ, "for ye are all one in Christ Jesus. And if ye be Christ's, then are ye Abraham's seed, and heirs according to the promise" (Gal. 3:28-29).

This sequence is identified so strikingly in Peter's sermon on the day of Pentecost. "Therefore [Jesus] being by the right hand of God exalted, and having received of the Father the promise of the Holy Ghost, he [Jesus] hath shed forth this which ye now see and hear" (Acts 2:33).

Christ, the Head of the Church, and in behalf of the Church, received the promise. Having received the promise, He then gave Him to the Church. The 120 were the first members of His body, the Church, to receive the promise of the Father, but they were by no means to be the last. For Peter, anointed mightily by the Holy Spirit, after the initial 120 had received, extended the promise from then until now, when he declared, "For the promise is unto you, and to your children, and to all that are afar off, even as many as the Lord our God shall call" (Acts 2:39).

Before concluding this chapter, something must be said further about the inheritance aspect of the promise of the Father.

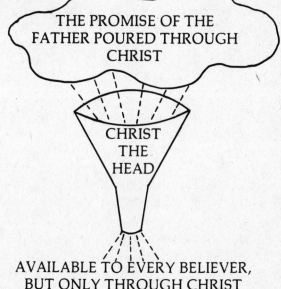

THE PROMISE OF THE
FATHER POURED THROUGH
CHRIST

CHRIST
THE
HEAD

AVAILABLE TO EVERY BELIEVER,
BUT ONLY THROUGH CHRIST

While the processes of fulfillment of the promises made to Abraham were occurring to natural Israel, there was first an earnest, and then there was the full inheritance.

The earnest, that is, the grapes of Eshcol brought out of Canaan by the spies, was by no means the whole inheritance. Nevertheless, it was a beautiful demonstration of that inheritance. While it was not the inheritance it was most assuredly the same in essence.

Canaan, with all its resources, with all its grapes and grain, with all its milk and honey, with all of its riches and rest, was the inheritance.

The promise of the Father for spiritual Israel, as for natural Israel, comprehends first the earnest of the inheritance, and then the inheritance itself in all its fullness.

The earnest is the fullness of the Holy Spirit. Yet it is only a glimpse of the fullness of the inheritance, though it too is the same in essence.

In the baptism in the Spirit, God shares himself with us in a unique and special way. When we are filled with the Spirit, it can be rightly said we are filled with God. This then becomes a clue to our full inheritance, wherein God will share himself with us beyond anything remotely possible in our earthly state, and not for only a brief span of years, but for eternity. Oh, joyful and glorious prospect!

No wonder the Psalmist cried, "The Lord is the portion of mine inheritance" (Ps. 16:5).

The question is, Have you received the Holy Ghost, the earnest of your inheritance?

thirteen

Tongues and Worship

In chapter 2 reasons were considered as to why tongues is, in many respects, the greatest gift of the Spirit. Among the seven reasons given was the reason of worship. Satan has done a master stroke of business in blinding the Church to this understanding. Therefore it seems important that more be said about it.

Tongues is vital to worship. Little wonder it has suffered such violence. Worship could well be its essential function. It is doubtful if the mountain peaks of worship are ever reached apart from it. Through tongues the human spirit is enabled to glorify God in a manner transcending any other means or ability.

The Church has no greater need than to learn true worship. According to the enlightened understanding of A.W. Tozer, "If Bible Christianity is to survive the present world upheaval, we shall need to recapture the spirit of worship. We shall need to have a fresh revelation of the greatness of God and the beauty of Jesus. We shall need to put away our phobias and our prejudices against the deeper life and seek again to be filled with the Holy Spirit. He alone can raise our cold hearts to rapture and restore again the art of worship."[22]

The charismatic community has already discovered worship. Yet the full meaning of the discovery may not be discerned or perceived. Worship through tongues is the Spirit's mighty answer to modern man's subtle temptation to idolatry. "When the enemy shall come in like a flood, the Spirit of the Lord shall lift up a standard against him" (Isa. 59:19).

Idolatry is man's number-one problem. It confronts all of us, even us charismatics. If the charismatic Corinthians had the problem, we can expect it too. To them Paul wrote, "Neither be ye idolaters" (1 Cor. 10:7). And "flee from idolatry" (1 Cor. 10:14).

None of us would think of hewing an idol of wood or graving one of metal. Our temptation is more subtle. Ours is to make *ourselves* gods—to put ourselves ahead of God. This is idolatry of the most devastating kind. "Thou shalt have no other gods before me" (Exod. 20:3). To place self before God is to commit idolatry.

Unwitting America is a land of idolaters. At every turn of the way the temptation presents itself. Our educational system is shot through with it. The bombardment of humanism, the doctrines of self-expression and situation ethics, is unrelenting. Idolatry is bred into us. Our children are fed this diet from their earliest years. Self is the mighty center of everything. Rights and liberation movements abound. It all adds up to idolatry.

There is only one answer. Put God back at the center. "Thou shalt love the Lord thy God with all thy heart, and with all thy soul, and with all thy mind. This is the first and great commandment" (Matt. 22:37-38).

Worship God! That is the antidote for idolatry. Though idolatry infects our land, and even our churches, the Spirit of God has unveiled the answer. An unparalleled spirit of worship is on the move. We need only move with the Holy Spirit and we will escape idolatry.

True worship is a thing of the spirit. "But the hour cometh, and now is, when the true worshippers shall worship the Father in spirit and in truth: for the Father seeketh such to worship him. God is a Spirit: and they that worship him must worship him in spirit and in truth" (John 4:23-24).

Tongues is the blessed language of the sanctified spirit. When the Holy Spirit is allowed to indwell and fill the human spirit as He desires, muteness flees away. It is then that "out of his belly shall flow rivers of living water" (John 7:38). And worship becomes a thing of the spirit.

Think of the day of Pentecost. For the first time in history the Holy Spirit had fallen upon the Church. Human spirits came under the control and sway of the Holy Spirit. They all spoke with tongues. They spoke of the wonderful works of God. They worshiped like they had never before worshiped.

There was a repeat performance at Cornelius' house. There, too, the Bible says, "the Holy Ghost fell on all who heard the word" (Acts 10:44). And when He did, they worshiped. "For they heard them speak with tongues and magnify God" (Acts 10:46).

For too long the Church has been blinded to the God-intended role of tongues. It has suffered violence even in the house of its friends. We have assigned to it responsibilities never intended. It has been made by some a gift for guidance. Others have employed it for reprimand and judgment. Many have made it a vehicle whereby God speaks to His people. How is it that we have not seen it as the worship gift? "For he that speaketh in an unknown tongue speaketh not unto men, but unto God: for no man understandeth him: howbeit in the spirit he speaketh mysteries" (1 Cor. 14:2).

O church of God, learn to worship, learn to worship in the spirit. Use your Spirit-freed tongue to magnify the Lord. Then you will fulfill the greatest commandment of all, and idolatry will flee away.

Appendix

A Five-Step Sequence

(While some of the material in this chapter is also in chapter 9, the message is quite different. It is my prayer that the reader will gain extra insight and profit by reading it.)

In every outpouring of the Holy Spirit, for which a measure of evidence is retrievable, there is a common and recognizable pattern—an identifiable five-step sequence of events:

1) Evident spiritual hunger
2) Outpouring of the Holy Spirit upon receptive souls
3) Manifestation of utterance gifts
4) Abuse and/or misuse of those gifts
5) Correction of abuses and/or misuses, or disintegration and collapse of the group or movement

Since it is doubtful that any group of significant proportion has escaped a single step in the sequence, an overview of these notable outpourings will provide some valuable lessons both for the present moment and for the unborn future.

We will begin with the original outpouring of the Holy Spirit as recorded in Acts. It is not difficult to discern the spiritual hunger of that momentous hour. Nor is it difficult to perceive that God foresaw the prevailing climate of that day when He scheduled it for Pentecost.

Longstanding spiritual drought tends to spawn spiritual hunger, and spiritual hunger creates the vacuum into which the Holy Spirit so easily enters. "Blessed are they which do hunger and thirst after righteousness: for they shall be filled" (Matt. 5:6).

For four hundred years Israel had been at a spiritual low. Isaiah had foreseen the resulting spiritual desert when he prophesied and identified the Messiah as "a root out of a dry ground" (Isa. 53:2). It was this fearful climate of drought which seemed to set the stage for that first Pentecostal outpouring.

Multitudes began to hunger for something beyond the meager fare afforded by the now-stale types and shadows and ceremonies of a religion that seemed more dead than alive. They swarmed to the Jordan to hear John the Baptist. They thronged Jesus as if desperate for a ray of light and hope. And, as if to climax that spirit of hunger, 120 of them secluded themselves in an upper room for ten days, demonstrating the genuineness and intensity of their desire.

Then came God's response. The Holy Spirit was poured upon them in a fashion unknown to the previous history of man.

And quick on the heels of that first outpouring came the third step in the sequence—the manifestation of the utterance gifts. For "they began to speak with other tongues, as the Spirit gave them utterance" (Acts 2:4).

But what about the fourth step? Was there abuse and/or misuse of those gifts in the early Church? Yes indeed. Even in the Acts there are hints at abuse or misuse. (Note my comments in the chapter entitled, "Utterance Gifts for Guidance.") But certainly abuse and/or misuse was present at Corinth.

How does step five apply to the early church? Beautifully! Corinth is the prime example. True, the church there fell victim to abuses and misuses, particularly of the tongues gift. But Paul was their salvation. Surely he was God's inspired instrument to correct the areas of error, as he did in 1 Corinthians 12 through 14. His teachings and guidelines so turned them around that he later wrote to the same church in highest commendation, "Therefore . . . ye abound in everything, in faith, and utterance [likely properly ordered supernatural utterance], and knowledge, and in all diligence, and in your love to us . . ." (2 Cor. 8:7). Thus, instead of disintegrating because of their improper manifestations, sound teaching preserved them and paved the pathway to coveted spiritual heights.

Next to be appraised is the Montanist movement. It was born in the second century after Christ, and it was Pentecostal in nature.

What precipitated this movement? Again the evidence points to spiritual hunger. It is noteworthy that the Church is cyclic, just as Israel was cyclic in her spiritual pursuits. The spiritual ups and downs of Israel, though utterly deplorable, cannot be ignored. Israel was as fickle as the wind. Led by a godly king, they would serve God for a period, enjoying His bounties. But let that king die, and another, with an ungodly bent replace him, and Israel would rush into idolatry as if she had never had a breath of spiritual perception or interest.

Sadly enough, the Church has not been too different. Only a few decades had passed when the Church, which had been launched in the full glory of Pentecost, was groveling in the dust of a spiritual desert. Remember how Jesus, through His servant John on Patmos, deplored the conditions prevailing in several of the churches in Asia Minor. ". . . thou hast left thy first love" (Rev. 2:4); "I have a few things against thee" (2:14, 20); ". . . thou hast a name that thou livest, and art dead" (3:1); "So then because thou art lukewarm, I will spue thee out of my mouth" (3:16). And that was prior to A.D. 100!

Little wonder then that hunger was born anew in the hearts of men who must have heard of Pentecost's glory, but who themselves knew only the dry bones of a deceased glory.

Then came Montanus—and in Asia Minor! Who can question that he hungered for God, and experienced an outpouring of the Holy Spirit so great that historians could not forget him? Nor was he alone in his experience, for a sizable following developed, encompassing even one so great as the mighty Tertullian.

History, though it is not overly complimentary, does underscore the presence of the supernatural gifts of utterance among those people. *The Pulpit Commentary*, for example, in discussing 1 Cor. 14:2, observes, "The whole of this chapter proves in a most striking way the close analogy between 'the tongue' and the impassioned soliloquies of inarticulate utterance which were poured forth in tones of thrilling power among the Montanists. . ."[23]

That there were abuses and/or misuses of the gifts is all too evident. H.M. Evans says that "He [Tertullian] and those who joined him were associated with the churches of the New Prophecy, and apparently read the oracles of these prophets along with other Christian writing circulated at this time."[24] We wonder if they resorted to their own prophetic utterances above the Scriptures, or whether they were led down the danger-fraught path of guidance by utterance gifts. Perhaps they had problems in both areas.

At any rate, it is quite evident that the Montanist movement planted the seeds of its own undoing at step five. We can only guess the reason, though some signals seem rather clear. A grave danger lurks in the shadows of every mighty work of God. Jesus had barely appeared as an innocent and helpless babe, when "the old dragon" stood by to devour the Child. Thus it has always been. And there is reason to believe that the Montanists were no exception. Could it be that subtle spiritual pride springing up on the heels of glorious manifestations of supernatural power influenced the leadership to assume a spiritual superiority, thus blinding them to the Pauline guidelines and directives which were intended for their preservation and prosperity? I believe so.

In any event, the Montanists fell into disrepute and the movement disintegrated.

Hastening through the centuries, we confront another significant Pentecostal outpouring. It occurred in connection with the ministry and leadership of Edward Irving in Great Britain and became known as the Irvingite movement.

Edward Irving was born in 1792. By 1815 he was a licentiate in the Church of Scotland, and in 1819 he became assistant in St. John's parish in Glasgow.

While secular scholars tend to state facts as they perceive them, it is doubtful that they could perceive what generated the Pentecostal thrust of Irving and his followers. They might easily credit the experience to a taste for the novel and spectacular, and at the same time overlook a hunger and thirst incited on the one hand by stagnant religiosity and on the other by spiritual insights growing out of attention to the Scriptures.

One thing is certain, Irving and his followers experienced an outpouring of the Holy Spirit, along with supernatural manifestations of tongues and prophecy. One historian states that in 1832 charges were preferred against Irving in connection with the so-called "unknown tongues." Such a course of action might be expected, for at that point in history theological perceptions relating to such supernatural manifestations were at a low ebb.

Yet the disintegration of the Irvingite movement can be traced to other causes. From sketchy information available it is apparent that the Irvingites, as is the usual case with all Pentecostal groups, did not escape step four. Abuses and/or misuses of the utterance gifts, particularly prophecy, set in. Prophecy was resorted to for personal direction and guidance, and evidently got out of hand.

We wonder why some able teacher could not have led them in right paths. But perhaps the truths which could have helped were so deeply buried under a maze of theological interpretations and taboos that they could not be discovered.

So the Irvingite movement, though its flame burned brightly for a short moment, smoldered and died.

The birth of the classical Pentecostal movement came less than one hundred years after the demise of the Irvingites. Again the five-step sequence is undeniably present.

Several factors seemed to unite in setting the stage for a spiritual awakening as the nineteenth century was nearing its end. Christianity had fallen upon hard times. Spiritual sterility was widespread. Unitarianism had affected vast areas of the Christian world. And Darwinism had its vicious tentacles around the jugular vein of Fundamentalism.

But while it was a rather fearful hour for vital Christianity, it also proved to be a most blessed hour; for around the world an intense hunger for God was born. Not a few are persuaded that this is what precipitated the beginning of the "latter rain" which would ripen the "harvest" at the end of the Church age.

In any event, as the new century was making its debut,

the Holy Spirit was being experienced in a new way worldwide. Groups far removed from each other and totally uninfluenced by each other discovered a common and revolutionizing dimension in the Holy Spirit.

And, true to the pattern, as these peoples were filled with the Spirit, they began to manifest the utterance gifts—tongues, interpretation and prophecy.

Nor did they, by any stretch of the imagination, avoid abuse and/or misuse of these gifts.

My contact with Pentecostals began in the early 1930s, and I am personally conversant with some of the questionable practices and child's play that happened. For example, my home church, on a given Sunday morning, had twenty-two "messages in tongues and interpretations"! I think God smiled, and winked at their ignorance.

Excesses were not uncommon, but we dare not succumb to the temptation to write off all manifestations of utterance gifts as senseless and meaningless, merely because there may be some abuses and misuses. How much better to discover right uses and gain the valuable benefits.

The classical Pentecostals did just that. While many earlier Pentecostals, as has been previously shown, failed utterly at step five in the sequence, the classical Pentecostal movement survived with flying colors. The reason is obvious. Able teachers, such as Donald Gee, Myer Pearlman, W.I. Evans, P.C. Nelson, to name only a few, rose up, even as Paul in his day, to establish biblical guidelines, point out dangers, and give general and sound direction. And they were heeded, with the result that the movement now covers the earth, numbering in the millions, and is recognized as the third force in Christendom.

A final demonstration of the five-step sequence can be witnessed in the charismatic movement, which had its beginnings in the late 1950s and early 1960s.

Seed produces its own harvest. While the classical Pentecostals faithfully planted, they often found the soil unreceptive. Old-line denominations tended to write them off as emotional, fanatical, extremists. They were sometimes classed with the cults. They were written against, preached against, denounced, and called "of the devil." But they went on planting.

Then it began to happen. Light penetrated the darkness. Hunger sprang up most remarkably. Protestants and Catholics alike hungered. Behind the walls of monasteries and convents, they hungered. In the old-line denominations it was no different. In schools of higher learning and among the twice-lost youth who wandered aimlessly, it happened. The rich and the poor, the young and the older, the religious and the nonreligious—strangely they began to hunger.

Were they to be disappointed? By no means. "Blessed are they which do hunger." Indeed they were blessed, for upon them the Holy Spirit has fallen in a measure beyond even the fondest dreams of earlier Pentecostals. Catholics, Episcopalians, Methodists, Lutherans, Baptists, Presbyterians and hosts of others—many of them began to speak with other tongues and manifest other gifts of the Spirit.

Have they successfully avoided step four? No. Like all other groups upon which the Holy Spirit has fallen in Pentecostal fashion, they too have been unable to suddenly and totally rise to all the glorious heights of spiritual manifestation apart from a learning process. And, as is quite normal, the problem area is utterance gifts—tongues, interpretation, prophecy. In some instances zealous souls have attempted to teach others to speak with tongues, and some who have been ministered to in that way have been disillusioned and disappointed. We dare not be too critical at this point, however, for there is a fine line between human manipulation and sincere encouragement of faith.

Some have resorted to the utterance gifts for guidance and direction and have failed to discern between the human spirit and the Holy Spirit. Others have transcribed prophetic utterances and have circulated them.

What will the outcome be? That depends almost totally on step five. Either there will be correction of the abuses and misuses by the application of biblical guidelines, or the charismatic movement will lose its thrust and fade away. The outcome will be determined for the most part by the charismatics themselves. If they will be responsive to the Scriptures, to able Bible teachers, and to the voice of experience, they will continue to bless the world. Otherwise they will hasten to their demise.

Notes

1. Donald Gee, *Concerning Spiritual Gifts* (Nottingham, England: Assemblies of God Publishing House), pp. 106-14. Used by permission.

2. Harold Horton, *The Gifts of the Spirit*, 10th ed. (Nottingham, England: Assemblies of God Publishing House, 1971), p. 140. Used by permission.

3. *The Pulpit Commentary, First Epistle to the Corinthians* (London and New York: Funk and Wagnalls Co., Wartime Edition), p. 457.

4. *Defender* magazine (Wichita, Kan., n.d.).

5. Anthony Hoekema, *What About Tongues Speaking?* (Grand Rapids, Mich.: William B. Eerdmans Publishing Co., 1966), p. 68. Used by permission.

6. Ibid. Used by permission.

7. Dennis J. Bennett, *Nine O'Clock in the Morning* (Plainfield, N.J.: Logos International, 1970), pp. 23-24. Used by permission.

8. *The Pulpit Commentary*, p. 458.

9. Ibid.

10. *The Pulpit Commentary, Epistle to the Romans*, p. 211.

11. Ibid.

12. Horton, *Gifts*, pp. 146-47. Used by permission.

13. John Sherrill, *They Speak With Other Tongues* (Westwood, N.J.: Fleming H. Revell, 1966).

14. *The Pulpit Commentary, The Book of the Prophet Isaiah*, p. 449.

15. *Pentecostal Evangel*, December 18, 1943. Used by permission of the General Council of the Assemblies of God, Springfield, Mo.

16. *Paraclete*, Fall 1975. Used by permission of Gospel Publishing

House, Springfield, Mo.

17. Ibid.

18. *Paraclete,* Winter 1971. Used by permission.

19. Horton, *Gifts,* p. 145. Used by permission.

20. *Pentecostal Evangel,* August 7, 1966. Used by permission.

21. Dick Eastman, *The Purple Pig and Other Miracles* (Monroeville, Pa.: Whitaker House, 1974), pp. 149-50. Used by permission.

22. A.W. Tozer, *That Incredible Christian* (Harrisburg, Pa.: Christian Publishers, Inc., 1964), p. 131.

23. *The Pulpit Commentary, Corinthians,* p. 457.

24. *Paraclete,* Fall 1975. Used by permission.